THE CRISIS OF THE UNION

1860–1861

The Crisis
of the Union

1860-1861

Edited by

GEORGE HARMON KNOLES

Louisiana State University Press

1965

The chapter by Professor Avery Craven, "Why the Southern States Seceded," published initially in a collection of
his essays entitled *An Historian and the Civil War,* is used
with the permission of the University of Chicago Press.

PREFACE

The Institute of American History had its legal birth on December 17, 1942, when the Board of Trustees of Stanford University approved a proposal initiated by Edgar E. Robinson, then Margaret Byrne Professor of American History and executive head of the Department of History. The Institute was organized to conduct conferences of teachers and scholars, to promote research, and to support publication of materials. During its early years the Institute sponsored a number of conferences devoted to the subject matter of American history. Faculty members from California universities, colleges, and secondary schools gathered to discuss such questions as "What is the content of American history?" and "What should be the function of teachers and scholars in defining the content of American history taught in the schools, colleges, and universities?"

In 1952 the Institute conducted a summer workshop on the historical bases of Americanism. The conference held in the summer of 1955 explored the problem of the individual in history with sessions devoted to the roles of biography, literature, and the arts in American history.

During the winter of 1961–62 the Institute discussed the feasibility of holding a conference on the subject of the Civil War. As our discussions developed, we decided to hold such a meeting and to direct attention to the crisis of the union, 1860–61. We asked a group of scholars to present papers and comments dealing with the following problems: "Why the Republican party came to power," "Why the Democratic party divided," "Why the Southern states seceded," and "Why the Republicans rejected both compromise and secession."

Following several weeks of planning we assembled our panel of participants from among those American historians who had wrestled with the questions which the failure of party government in the United States during the 1850's had posed for the serious student of American history. To the conference we invited other scholars and teachers of American history; some five hundred attended the four sessions conducted at Stanford University on March 1–2, 1963.

For those who participated in the conference as well as for that larger audience concerned with trying to unravel the tangled threads of action and motivation leading to the crisis of the union, the Institute is pleased to offer this volume. Readers will find presented here in stimulating and challenging manner theses and views of a select company of historians who have devoted the major portion of their professional careers to a study of the forces and men involved in the developments leading to the American Civil War.

Again I would like to thank Professors Avery Craven, Don E. Fehrenbacher, Robert W. Johannsen, Roy F. Nichols, David M. Potter, Charles G. Sellers, Jr., Kenneth M. Stampp, and Glyndon G. Van Deusen for their provocative papers, for their part in making our conference the great success that it was, and for making this volume possible. To Professors Thomas A. Bailey and John C. Miller and to Emeritus Professor Edgar E. Robinson I owe thanks for their able assistance in chairing and moderating sessions of the conference. Finally, I wish to thank Miss Lisette Fast and Mrs. Jane Morgan, secretary and assistant secretary of the Institute, for their invaluable aid in the planning and staging of the conference and in the preparation of the papers for publication.

London, England
July 8, 1964

GEORGE HARMON KNOLES
Professor of History and
Director, Institute of
American History,
Stanford University

CONTENTS

THE CRISIS OF THE UNION

1860–1861

I

WHY THE REPUBLICAN PARTY CAME TO POWER

Glyndon G. Van Deusen

It is generally accepted that the Republican party came into existence as a direct consequence of the passage of the Kansas-Nebraska Act of 1854. The old parties had already begun to crumble. The new party emerged, not as the result of careful planning or around one outstanding leader, but out of "Free Soil Leagues," anti-Nebraska clubs, the formation of hundreds of committees, and the calling of local and state conventions throughout the North. Right or wrong, millions of Northerners felt that they were confronted by the prospect of slavery spreading into a vast area of the West. To a considerable number, this meant perpetuation of the South's political control of the national government and its economic policies; the frustration of Northern desires for internal improvements, free homesteads, financial reforms, and a higher tariff. To others, and they were many, it meant a new lease on life for the moral degradation of slavery. To all, as Horace Greeley once remarked, it was as though Macbeth's awful warning, "Sleep no more," resounded throughout the land "in thundertones that would not die unheeded." [1] The Republicans invoked the name of Jefferson and took their title

1 Horace Greeley, *Recollections of a Busy Life* (New York, 1868), 294; Herbert Agar, *The Price of Union* (Boston, 1950), 357, 373–75; Wilfred Ellsworth Binkley, *American Political Parties* (New York, 1959), 207.

from the party founded by the Sage of Monticello, himself no friend of the peculiar institution.

But though the party emerged with a blowing of trumpets, it seemed doomed to a short and uneasy life. Stephen A. Douglas said it would vanish into thin air, and there was good reason for such prophecy. Unlike the preceding major parties, it was sectional; its distribution was uneven, its greatest initial strength being in rural areas of Massachusetts, Vermont, western New York, and northeastern Ohio. It had no seasoned state and interstate organization with reliable financial backing. From the start it was a heterogeneous mixture of diverse and uneasy elements that ranged from opponents of slavery, or slavery extension, to temperance advocates hoping to use it in their battle against Demon Rum. While some politicians like Charles Sumner, Salmon P. Chase, Francis P. Blair, Sr., and Gideon Welles came early into the fold, others such as Abraham Lincoln, Thurlow Weed, William H. Seward, and Simon Cameron cautiously held back. In Massachusetts, Henry Wilson tells us, the movement at first attracted no prominent Whigs or Democrats. In Pennsylvania, the first Republican state convention was held in September, 1855, but attempted fusion with the Whigs and Americans was only partially successful; the Democrats won an easy victory that fall.

Despite all difficulties, however, the party achieved national organization and made an impressive record in the 1856 campaign. Although John Charles Frémont could best be described as a showman rather than a statesman, he polled 33.1 per cent of the popular vote, and had 114 electoral votes to Buchanan's 174. Republicanism swept New England, New York, Ohio, Michigan, Iowa, and Wisconsin and made impressive inroads in the other Northern states. The Democrats carried hardly a county north of the 41st parallel, a line running roughly through the central portions of New Jersey, Pennsylvania, Ohio, Indiana, and Illinois. The new party had been unable to win Pennsylvania, New Jersey, Indiana, and Illinois and was practically nonexistent south of the Mason-Dixon line; but it was equally apparent that the nativist American party, which had had a mushroom growth and was hopeful of victory, had obtained only 21.6 per cent of the popular vote. If this decline continued and if inroads could be made in Democratic

Northern strongholds, Republican prospects for victory in 1860 would be bright.[2]

The unstable character of the Republican party, however, was still one of its principal characteristics. Professor A. N. Holcombe estimates that in 1856 it had in its ranks a smattering of abolitionists, one Free-Soiler out of every six or seven members, former Whigs and Democrats in proportions of approximately four to one, and a very considerable number of new voters. Temperance advocates and naturalized citizens attracted by the "equality of rights" plank in the 1856 platform further complicated the situation.[3] How could this conglomeration achieve a position of power?

A variety of factors contributed to the increasing strength of the Republican party during the next four years. Millard Fillmore, the Whig-American fusion candidate of 1856, had carried only Maryland, and the nativist uprising collapsed as swiftly as it arose. The American party had no fundamental issue in the foreign bogey, and Northerners and Southerners split over slavery. Southern Whigs and Know-Nothings tended to move into the Democracy. More and more Northern Whigs and "Know-Somethings" moved into the Republican camp. This recruitment in numbers was an encouraging sign. The Republican party was youthful, hopeful, unburdened by an accumulation of mistakes over a long past; and it was finding strong leaders, whereas the Democrats, in both state and national governments, were plagued by feuds, corruption, and an increasingly bitter quarrel between Douglas and Buchanan over Kansas and its Lecompton constitution.[4]

A third factor in Republican strength was the increasing Northern discontent with the economic policies of the Democratic party and its Southern backers. The South opposed free land, internal improvements, and a higher tariff, all of which were popular in the North; Southerners also controlled the most important committees

2 Walter Dean Burnham, *Presidential Ballots, 1836–1892* (Baltimore, 1955), 64–71.
3 Arthur Norman Holcombe, *The Political Parties of Today* (New York, 1924), 172; Andrew Wallace Crandall, *The Early History of the Republican Party, 1854–1856* (Boston, 1930), *passim*.
4 Roy F. Nichols, *The Disruption of American Democracy* (New York, 1948), 202–26; Reinhard Henry Luthin, *The First Lincoln Campaign* (Cambridge, 1944), 17, 120–35.

in both House and Senate. Pierce, and then Buchanan, bowed to Southern wishes; and when a bill disliked by the South did run the congressional gauntlet, it received short shrift at the White House. Pierce alone vetoed five rivers and harbors bills; three times in eight years Democratic votes defeated free homestead bills in the Senate; and particularly irksome was Buchanan's veto of the homestead bill of 1860. To make matters still worse, Old Buck, at the behest of speculators and Southern supporters, in 1858, 1859, and 1860 ordered over 46,000,000 acres of public lands into the market at a time when 80,000,000 acres were already available for sale. This was a bitter blow to the squatters in Kansas, Iowa, Wisconsin, and other parts of the West, all the more bitter because, in the spring of 1860, the Senate Democrats defeated a House bill that would have prevented anyone but actual settlers from acquiring public lands until ten years after their survey. This offended both Northern farmers and Northern labor.[5]

The tariff of 1857 and the depression of that same year were also grist for the Republican mill. Greeley, on his annual lecture tour in early 1858, found many evidences of protectionist sentiment in the West. In May of 1860, Justin S. Morrill's bill raising rates to the old Walker tariff level had all the free state votes but fourteen, yet could muster only eight votes from the slave states.[6] Small wonder that, when a Southern-guided Democracy prevented the raising of tariffs, blocked internal improvements at federal expense and the free distribution of public lands while it maintained the Independent Treasury, penalized squatters, and held up the admission of states, the North and West should come to the conclusion that there was a "Slave Power" which controlled the government and was determined to prevent the economic development of its Northern neighbors.[7]

At the same time Republicanism fed on economic discontent

5 Paul Wallace Gates, "The Struggle for Land and the 'Irrepressible Conflict,'" *Political Science Quarterly,* LXVI (June, 1951), 248–71; John Rogers Commons, "Horace Greeley and the Working Class Origins of the Republican Party, *"Political Science Quarterly,* XXIV (September, 1909), 468–88; Luthin, *The First Lincoln Campaign,* 12–14; Roy F. Nichols, "1461–1861: The American Civil War in Perspective," *Journal of Southern History,* XVI (May, 1950), 155–56.
6 Jeter Allen Isely, *Horace Greeley and the Republican Party, 1853–1861* (Princeton, 1947), 222; Luthin, *The First Lincoln Campaign,* 7.
7 Nichols, "1461–1861: The American Civil War in Perspective," 156;

with the Democracy and the "Slave Power," it also derived sustenance from antislavery sentiment based on moral grounds. Morality judgments carried great weight one hundred years ago. Religious teachings made a deep impact during the 1850's: Northern pastors of evangelical churches thought they knew a sin when they saw one, and both preachers and congregations knew that slavery was sinful.[8] How else can one account for the instant and continuing popularity of Harriet Beecher Stowe's *Uncle Tom's Cabin;* or the violent reaction to the Kansas-Nebraska bill, which prompted Douglas to say he could travel from New England to Illinois by the light of his burning effigies; or the agitation over Kansas and the Lecompton and English bills; or the anger over the caning of Sumner and the enduring controversy over whether he was shamming that kept alive the passions roused in 1856;[9] or the near-deification of John Brown; or the personal liberty laws enacted in state after state; or the underground railway and the rescue of imprisoned fugitives? Granted that some of this was deliberately stirred up by Republican politicians and the Republican press; granted that they kept Kansas "bleeding" for political advantage;[10] granted that some Republicans were politicans first and men of principle afterward, and even that antislavery leaders were frustrated men seeking outlets for their energy and ambitions: there remains the phenomenon of a sectional party that rallied to its ranks hundreds of thousands of persons who believed that slavery was morally wrong; a party, many of whose adherents did care whether slavery was voted up or voted down; one whose members felt the deep injustice of white men having the arbitrary power to make black men stand in fear and who spoke in terms of a "higher law," an "irrepressible conflict," and a "house divided."

There remains still another factor that helps account for the increasing strength of the Republican party: the increasing gap between the sections. Moral passion, distorted news, a sense of

Avery O. Craven, "The Price of Union," *Journal of Southern History,* XVIII (February, 1952), 5.
8 Professor Craven has suggested the importance of religious assistance to the Republican party in his *The Growth of Southern Nationalism, 1848–1861* (Baton Rouge, 1953), 187–88.
9 Laura Amanda White, "Was Charles Sumner Shamming?" *New England Quarterly,* XXXIII (September, 1960), 291–324.
10 James Claude Malin, *John Brown and the Legend of Fifty-Six* (Philadelphia, 1942), 89–116, 211–45.

economic injury, and a succession of calamitous events had made it difficult, if not impossible, for the average Northerner to comprehend or appreciate the enormous problem that the Negro was to the South. If there had been more of a spirit of compassion brought by recognition of the situation confronting the Southern whites, there would have been fewer converts to the ranks of the Republican party.

By 1860, then, the Republican party was in a position of great strength. For the past four years it had had a superb chairman of its national committee in Governor Edwin D. Morgan of New York, and it was well organized on a national basis. Its leading figures in key states—Seward and Weed in New York, John A. Andrew in Massachusetts, Andrew G. Curtin in Pennsylvania, Oliver P. Morton in Indiana, and Richard Yates in Illinois—were men of outstanding ability. Chase, William M. Evarts, George William Curtis, Carl Schurz, John Sherman, Lyman Trumbull, and Francis P. Blair, Jr., were effective speakers. A galaxy of great editors, among them Greeley, William Cullen Bryant, and Samuel Bowles; outstanding men of letters such as Emerson, Thoreau, Holmes, Whittier, and Lowell; and leaders in the fields of medicine, law, learning and theology constituted an impressive array of talent and intellectual power that the Democracy could not match.[11]

If the Republicans had talent on their side, they also showed political realism in the selection of a convention city and in the drafting of their platform. Chicago was chosen as neutral ground, since only Norman Judd on the national committee thought of Lincoln as a serious candidate for the nomination.[12] The platform drawn up at the convention was a blend of idealism and practicality, recognizing the necessity of raising a standard to which all the elements of the party could repair in their struggle with the Democracy. It denounced the extravagance and corruption of Democratic administration; it advocated protection, but not too much protection; it urged rivers and harbors appropriations, a Pa-

11   Allan Nevins, *The Emergence of Lincoln* (2 vols.; New York, 1950), II, 230–32, 299; A. M. Simon, *Social Forces in American History* (New York, 1914), 255–58.
12   Luthin, *The First Lincoln Campaign*, 21.

cific railroad, a daily overland mail, and a homestead law; it took a stand, but not in offensive language, against impairment of the immigrant's rights of citzenship.

Nor was the platform exactly mealymouthed in its attitude toward slavery. To be sure, it did not go as far as the 1856 platform which declared that Congress had the right and duty "to prohibit in the territories those twin relics of barbarism, polygamy and slavery," and it upheld the right of the states to order and control their own domestic institutions; but in no less than seven of its seventeen planks there was reference to the peculiar institution. It declared that the causes which had called the party into existence now demanded, more than ever, "its peaceful and constitutional triumph"; it asserted that the great principles of the Declaration of Independence—"that all men are created equal; that they are endowed by their Creator with certain unalienable rights"—must be maintained; it denounced the attempt "to force the infamous Lecompton constitution upon the protesting people of Kansas—"; it maintained that the "new dogma" that the Constitution carries slavery into any or all of the territories of the United States was a "dangerous political heresy—revolutionary in its tendency and subversive of the peace and harmony of the country"; it denied "the authority of Congress, a territorial legislature, or any individual to give legal existence to slavery in any territory of the United States"; it branded the reopening of the African slave trade as "a crime against humanity" and called for suppression of "that execrable traffic"; it upheld the right of the Kansas and Nebraska legislatures to exclude slavery from those territories and demanded the immediate admission of Kansas under a constitution prohibiting slavery.

The Republican platform of 1860 devoted considerably more space to slavery and the ramifications of the slavery problem than it did to such economic issues as the tariff, internal improvements, and free land. There was much in it to justify the antislavery voter in feeling that the Republican party was his natural and rightful home. In the words of Professor James A. Woodburn, "The spirit of the party [in 1860] was antislavery. Its purpose was to girdle the tree of slavery and let it die." [13]

13 James Albert Woodburn, *Political Parties and Party Problems in the United States* (Rev. ed.; New York, 1924), 107–108.

The stand taken by the Republican convention had appeal on both moral and economic grounds for the citizens of the North; yet it was not so extreme as to offend unduly those in or out of the party who were Know-Nothings, opponents of high protection, or conservatives fearing that rash action might provoke secession and civil war. The same may be said of its choice of a presidential candidate. Bargains, and to some extent sheer pandemonium, played a part in the selection of Abraham Lincoln; but the prime consideration was his availability.

We are not concerned here with why William Seward or Edward Bates or some other candidate was *not* chosen, but rather with why Lincoln was such a strong candidate. To begin with, Lincoln, as a Westerner and a log cabin rail-splitter, was a symbol of the common man and as such was bound to have vote appeal. He had also identified himself as a friend of labor, one who, at New Haven, had publicly approved the right to strike. He had carefully cultivated the foreign-born and was well-liked by the German element in the population.

Particularly significant was Lincoln's attitude toward the South and toward slavery. He had never denounced Southerners, as William L. Garrison, Sumner, and Greeley had done. In September, 1859, in a speech at Cincinnati, he had advocated putting a Southern man on the Republican presidential ticket; and in his Cooper Union speech, February 27, 1860, he had taken a conciliatory position, repudiating both Hinton R. Helper's attack on slavery and John Brown's raid on Harper's Ferry.[14] On slavery, too, his position was that of a moderate. Convinced that it was morally wrong, he clearly disliked it; but he was no immediate abolitionist, and he did not criticize the Southerners for defending their peculiar institution. His "House Divided" speech was not radical or revolutionary, but simply a statement that, once slavery extension in the territories was stopped, slavery would be on the way to an ultimate extinction that might take a long time to achieve, perhaps a century.[15]

14   Arthur Charles Cole, "President Lincoln and the Illinois Radical Republicans," *Mississippi Valley Historical Review,* IV (March, 1918), 419; James Garfield Randall, *The Civil War and Reconstruction* (New York, 1937), 178.
15   Don E. Fehrenbacher, *Prelude to Greatness* (Stanford, 1962), 70–95,

Lincoln also had useful personal connections. Himself a moderately conservative Whig who could be portrayed as of the Henry Clay stripe, his close friend and law partner, W. H. Herndon, was an abolitionist; and another friend and supporter was the former Democrat, Lyman Trumbull. There can be little doubt that the convention saw him as a uniting force for the coming campaign, for he was sufficiently in the middle so that all sides in the party could rally to him, each hoping eventually to control him. His moderation also made it likely that he would obtain votes from outside the Republican ranks, a prime consideration in the crucial Northern states.[16]

The Republicans went into the campaign of 1860 with an effective national organization and with high morale. The principal party leaders—Seward, Bates, Chase, Schurz, Cameron, and a score of others—rallied to the ticket. The Democracy was hopelessly split, with John C. Breckinridge the candidate of the Southern Democrats, and Douglas the standard bearer for the Democrats of the North. The Constitutional Unionists, a combination of Old Whigs and Know-Nothings pledged to solving the national crisis by ignoring it, had a lacklustre ticket with John Bell of Tennessee for President and Edward Everett of Massachusetts as his running mate. With the Democrats fighting bitterly among themselves, and the Constitutional Unionists seeking victory by evading issues, the Republicans had good reason to be confident.

One striking evidence of Republican morale was the organization of marching clubs known as the Wide Awakes. Originating in Hartford, Connecticut, when Cassius M. Clay came there in February, 1860, to deliver an address, the Wide Awakes spread all over the North and in a few months had some 400,000 members. Semimilitary, clad in uniforms, and carrying torches and colored lanterns, they quite outshone their rivals, the Bell-Ringers, the Little Giants, and the Breckinridge National Democratic Volunteers.[17]

108; T. Harry Williams, "Abraham Lincoln: Principle and Pragmatism in Politics: A Review Article," *Mississippi Valley Historical Review*, XL (June, 1953), 103; Luthin, *The First Lincoln Campaign, 72–73.*
16   David M. Potter, *Lincoln and His Party in the Secession Crisis* (New Haven, 1942), 34–35.
17   Luthin, *The First Lincoln Campaign,* 173–74; Emerson David Fite, *The Presidential Campaign of 1860* (New York, 1911), 225–26.

But enthusiasm was by no means the only Republican weapon in 1860. The campaign managers undertook to educate the public. The New York *Tribune* estimated that there were 10,000 Republican speeches made in New York state alone, and 50,000 in the nation. That paper also printed vast quantities of campaign material in cheap pamphlet form, notably a *Political Textbook for 1860,* of which Greeley was coeditor and which stated unblushingly that it conveyed the truth "without a trace of partisan bias." This sold at 66 cents a copy in quantity lots and by the first of October had gone into fourteen editions. Speeches by prominent Republicans were given wide circulation, and hundreds of thousands of copies of a pamphlet on the homestead bill were circulated in both German and English.[18]

There is every evidence that the Republicans used economic issues to advantage. They emphasized their free land plank in the Northwest and this, coupled with Buchanan's putting large areas of "squatter land" on the market and his veto of the homestead bill, brought heavy dividends. That Lincoln received 54 per cent of the total vote of Iowa, 56 per cent in Wisconsin, 57 per cent in Michigan, and 60 per cent in Minnesota was in considerable part due to the land issue. In Pennsylvania, New Jersey, and New England the tariff was used to advantage, and everywhere the changes were rung on internal improvements.[19] Labor was wooed by means of the tariff and homestead propaganda; by quotes from George Fitzhugh's *Sociology for the South,* which suggested the advisability of reducing free workingmen to a slave status; by circulating a Henry Wilson speech attacking Senator James H. Hammond for his characterization of laborers as the "mudsills of society"; and by using as a slogan the question, "How can the laboring man ever get two dollars a day when a black slave costs his master only ten cents a day?" [20]

Some historians have assumed that Northern labor trooped

18   Nevins, *The Emergence of Lincoln,* II, 302; Glyndon G. Van Deusen, *Horace Greeley: Nineteenth Century Crusader* (Philadelphia, 1953), 253.
19   Gates, "The Struggle for Land and the 'Irrepressible Conflict,' " 271; Nevins, *The Emergence of Lincoln,* II, 298–306; Luthin, *The First Lincoln Campaign,* 178, 187–88, 193–216.
20   Binkley, *American Political Parties,* 219, 231.

into the Republican ranks.[21] There is evidence, however, that by no means all laborers voted the Republican ticket, for Lincoln's percentage of the popular vote was decidedly lighter in the urban areas of New England, New York, New Jersey, and Pennsylvania (save for the region around Pittsburgh) than it was in the rural parts of that region.[22] The same evidence, together with the investigations of Philip Foner, indicate that the major part of the business class was anti-Republican and that the "incorporated avarice" of industrial capitalism had something less than enthusiasm for the party of Abraham Lincoln.[23] The greatest strength of Republicanism lay in the small towns and on the farms of the North.

Professor Joseph Schafer found evidence that the Germans in Wisconsin did not vote for Lincoln, primarily because of the Know-Nothing element in Republicanism. Most historians feel, however, that the influence of Carl Schurz, Gustave Koerner, Friedrich Kapp, and other prominent German-Americans; of nearly a hundred German, Swedish, and Norwegian journals; of Lincoln's letter to the *Staats Anzeiger* in opposition to withholding the ballot for two years from fully naturalized citizens; and of the Republican homestead and "rights of citizenship" planks brought the great bulk of German and Scandinavian voters into the Republican fold.[24]

Another Republican asset was the care they took to parry the charge that their victory would result in secession. Southern threats of disunion in 1856 had rallied many Whigs to Buchanan, especially in such crucial states as Pennsylvania. In 1860 these threats began earlier and were more plentiful, but the Republicans declared that these warnings had no real significance. Regardless of whether they were sincere in this, the net effect of such scornful

21 See Commons, "Horace Greeley and the Working Class Origins of the Republican Party," 468–88; Arthur Meier Schlesinger, *New Viewpoints in American History* (New York, 1922), 270–71.
22 Ollinger Crenshaw, "Urban and Rural Voting in the Election of 1860," in *Historiography and Urbanization,* ed. Eric Goldman (Baltimore, 1941), 43–63.
23 *Ibid.;* Philip Sheldon Foner, *Business and Slavery* (Chapel Hill, 1941), 177–79, 319–22.
24 See Joseph Schafer, "Who Elected Lincoln," *American Historical Review,* XLVII (October, 1941), 51–63; Luthin, *The First Lincoln Campaign,* 45, 59, 186–87; Nevins, *The Emergence of Lincoln,* II, 298–306.

comments as Seward's "Who's afraid?" together with frequent Southern menaces of dire action during the previous decade, was to minimize the possibility of secession as a reason for voting against Lincoln.[25]

Another dangerous possibility was fusion of the Douglas-Bell-Breckinridge tickets. If accomplished in one or more crucial states, it could throw the election into the House where it might be possible to elect Breckinridge. If no President could be chosen in the House, the safely Democratic Senate would then elect Breckinridge's running mate, Joseph Lane, as Vice-President; and he would become President by default on March 4, 1861.

Plans to win the election by such means were largely frustrated by the bitterness that existed between the followers of Douglas and Buchanan and the implacable hatreds aroused between the Southern rights doctrinaires who demanded a congressional slave code for the territories and the Douglasites who stood by their champion's view that the people of a territory should have the privilege of deciding for or against slavery. It is true that the Douglas and Breckinridge platforms hedged on this fundamental issue, the former agreeing to let the Supreme Court determine "the subject of domestic relations" in the territories, the latter merely stating that it was the duty of the federal government to protect "when necessary" the rights of persons and property in the territories. But these statements notwithstanding, neither side had any trust in the other. Douglas refused to withdraw after he was nominated, denounced schemes for so dividing the electoral vote as to bring the election into the House, and assailed Breckinridge as a secessionist. Breckinridge and his supporters branded Douglas as a traitor and semiabolitionist who had destroyed Democratic unity.

Such fusion as was achieved had very limited success. That of the Bell, Breckinridge, and Douglas men in New Jersey, though it put up an electoral ticket, was too late to secure more than a division of the state's electoral vote between Lincoln and Douglas;

25 Potter, *Lincoln and His Party in the Secession Crisis,* 2–11; Kenneth M. Stampp, *And the War Came* (Baton Rouge, 1950), 1–12; Nevins, *The Emergence of Lincoln,* II, 306; Isely, *Horace Greeley and the Republican Party, 1853–1861,* 296–98, 301–305; Van Deusen, *Horace Greeley: Nineteenth Century Crusader,* 252–53.

that of the Douglas and Bell forces in New York was ineffectual, as was the effort at bringing together the Douglas and Breckinridge factions in Pennsylvania.[26]

It is an open question as to whether a united opposition could have defeated Lincoln. The Douglas-Bell-Breckinridge votes, *as they were,* if cast for one candidate, would still have left Lincoln the victor with 169 electors, a majority of 35. But with only one opposing candidate, and that one on the Democratic ticket, Democratic morale would have been higher than it was; the Democracy could have posed as the peace party, and this would probably have cut into the Republican vote. A swing of conservatives to such a candidate might have ensured Lincoln's defeat. On the other hand, it probably would have been difficult for a candidate who had the support of the whole South to carry the requisite number of free states.[27]

One other aspect of the campaign remains to be examined—the Republican party's position on slavery. Was the slavery issue minimized by the Republicans? Did it, or did it not, play a significant role in the campaign? It is true that the tariff, internal improvements, and free land were given great importance in various sections of the North by the Republican speakers and the Republican press and that the general tone of both toward the South was moderate and conciliatory. Nevertheless, slavery as a moral question remained an extremely important part of the Republican campaign.

Lincoln had made clear repeatedly his conviction that slavery extension was a moral issue. He had done this in 1854 on the Kansas-Nebraska question, as well as on later occasions.[28] The

26 Luthin, *The First Lincoln Campaign,* 120–35, 225–26; Philip Shriver Klein, *President James Buchanan, a Biography* (University Park, Pa., 1962), 343–44, 347, 348; Don E. Fehrenbacher, "Lincoln, Douglas, and the Freeport Doctrine," *American Historical Review,* LXVI (April, 1961), 605, 610–11; Nichols, *The Disruption of American Democracy,* 341–44, 349–50; James Garfield Randall, *Lincoln the President* (2 vols.; New York, 1945), I, 195–98.
27 This possibility is discussed in Nevins, *The Emergence of Lincoln,* II, 312, and in Fehrenbacher, *Prelude to Greatness,* 159–60.
28 Roy Prentice Basler (ed.), *The Collected Works of Abraham Lincoln* (8 vols. and index; New Brunswick, N.J., 1953–1955), II, 222–23, 239, 353, 362, 405–406, 408; Nevins, *The Emergence of Lincoln,* I, 359–61; Fehren-

Republicans had nominated as their standard bearer a man who believed that slavery was an evil thing and that gradually but inexorably it must be abolished. There was, as we have seen, plenty of antislavery sentiment in the Republican platform. Even the homestead plank could be interpreted as antislavery—designed to increase the number of free states. The New York *Tribune* had for years excoriated slavery as a moral evil, and during the 1860 campaign Greeley told the readers of the *Independent* that the fundamental question was the ethics of slavery.[29] Republican leaders generally disapproved Sumner's speech in June, 1860, on "The Barbarism of Slavery"; but David Donald has pointed out that Sumner franked thousands of copies all over the country; by August the congressional Republican committee decided to circulate it at $2 a hundred. Copies of the speech were welcomed in rural districts of the North and West; by August Weed was begging Sumner to campaign in upstate New York, and the Senator from Massachusetts had already received urgent requests for speeches in Maine, Illinois, and Ohio.[30] H. R. Helper's *Impending Crisis* was also circulated as an antislavery campaign document.

Another interesting feature of the antislavery side of the Republican campaign is the character of Seward's speeches. One finds in them, on occasion, tributes to the foreign-born and references to the dignity and importance of free labor. He also stated emphatically the Republican party's reliance on moral suasion rather than force and the party's peaceful intent.[31] But in his speeches, whether in the West or in the East, there was little or no specific reference to the economic planks in the Republican platform. His central theme was slavery. He characterized it as opposed to a free system of government and as crippling to industry and commerce, both for the South and for the North. The past, he said, proved its expansionist tendency, an expansion that must be checked. He also

---

bacher, *Prelude to Greatness,* 108; Dwight Lovell Dumond, *Antislavery Origins of the Civil War in the United States* (Ann Arbor, 1939), 100; Avery O. Craven, *Civil War in the Making, 1815–1860* (Baton Rouge, 1959), 67.
29 Isely, *Horace Greeley and the Republican Party, 1853–1861,* 297; Van Deusen, *Horace Greeley: Nineteenth Century Crusader,* 213–21.
30 David Donald, *Charles Sumner and the Coming of the Civil War* (New York, 1960), 358, 361–65.
31 George E. Baker, *The Works of William H. Seward* (5 vols.; Boston, 1884–1889), IV, 334–37, 344–46, 360–66, 405, 415–21.

stated repeatedly that slavery was morally bad; that there was an "irrepressible conflict" between wrong and right, freedom and slavery; that past compromises with slavery had been of more than doubtful value. It was, he declared at St. Paul, "unjust and inhuman in its very nature—wrong and cruel—." [32]

While the Auburn statesman on more than one occasion declared that the North had freedom, and at Chicago assured his hearers that the great principles of the Declaration of Independence had "perfect acceptance" in eighteen states (including Kansas), he also came out at St. Paul for "absolute political equality" as a principle of government; asserted at Cleveland that "the right of all men to political equality is self-evident"; and later declared that freedom and equality meant freedom of speech, thought, suffrage, and religious conscience.[33]

That arch abolitionist, Charles Sumner, was delighted with Seward's efforts, the more so, probably, because he had earlier regretted his colleague's growing conservatism on slavery. Sumner wrote to Frances Seward that "at each speech, as I read it, I marvelled more and more," that the speech at Madison "was noble and went straight to my heart"; and he urged Seward to publish his campaign efforts in a single volume.[34] Far different was the reaction of "Two Minute Men" in Memphis, who sent to Auburn a cryptic warning—"For behold the end of all things is at hand." [35]

Seward had a great reception in the West; and Weed, Edwin D. Morgan, Richard M. Blatchford, and George E. Baker were enthusiastic about the success of his tour.[36] There is no evidence that these men felt he had overemphasized slavery at the expense of economic issues. And it is, I think, significant that in neither the Seward nor the Weed Papers is there any evidence of abolitionist

32 Ibid., IV, 310–14, 342–44, 348–58, 366–67, 373, 376–81, 384, 387, 390–92, 399, 404–407, 409, 412, 421, 422, 430.
33 Ibid., IV, 337, 384, 397–99.
34 Charles Sumner to Frances Seward, September 11, 18, October 10, 1860; Sumner to William H. Seward, October 10, 1860; in Seward Papers, University of Rochester, Rochester, New York.
35 "Two Minute Men" to Seward, November 4, 1860, in Seward Papers. This was the entire content of the note.
36 Richard M. Blatchford to Mrs. Seward, October 3, 1860; Edwin D. Morgan to Seward, October 6, 1860; George E. Baker to Seward, October 10, 1860; in Seward Papers.

discontent with Seward's speeches or with Republican policy. It is undoubtedly true that, in areas where antislavery sentiments were unpopular or of little interest, slavery was minimized by the Republicans; but this can hardly be said to have been the general character of the Republican campaign.

As the contest moved toward its close, omens appeared that were auspicious for the Republicans. The reelection of Missourian Francis P. Blair, Jr., to Congress in August, the first Republican Congressman from a slave state, encouraged the party to hope that it might win the border states. The subsequent Republican victories in Maine, Vermont, Pennsylvania, and Indiana inspirited the followers of Lincoln and dismayed the opposition, probably bringing some erstwhile Douglas supporters into the Republican camp.[37] Even so, when the national contest was over, Lincoln was a minority President, with only 39.9 per cent of the popular vote. His party also lacked a majority in both the House and the Senate until that situation was changed by the secession of the Southern states. But it had installed its chief in the White House and was in a position of great power.

Why were the Republicans victorious in the election of 1860? In other words, why did they win the electoral votes of the heavily populated Northern states and so capture the White House? As we have seen, there were a number of reasons for this result. The national party organization had become by 1860 a smooth and effective political machine. No bloc of potential Republican voters had any reason for disliking Lincoln. His public utterances had put him on record as antislavery, but not in favor of social and political equality for the Negro; he was sympathetic, but not in any violent fashion, with both the laboring man and the foreign-born. In short, he was an ideal candidate for a heterogeneous party composed, as Professor Hofstadter has rather acidly put it, of " 'abolitionists and Negrophobes, high- and low-tariff men, hard- and soft-money men, former Whigs and former Democrats, Maine-law prohibitionists and German tipplers, Know-Nothings and immigrants.' " [38]

37   Nevins, *The Emergence of Lincoln,* II, 300, 311.
38   Richard Hofstadter, *The American Political Tradition and the Men Who Made It* (New York, 1948), 117.

In addition to organization and candidate, the party profited by the discord among its opponents and by taking advantage of economic issues in the proper places. Times were good; the Northern economy, despite the temporary setback of 1857–58, was booming; appetite for gain was keen; and Southern leadership was negative where the North's economic development was concerned.

Another factor was the Republicans' skill in handling the possibility of secession and civil conflict. They minimized the danger, even treating it with derision; and this, together with reiterated declarations of peaceful intent, gave assurance to a Northern populace that wanted neither war nor the breakup of the Union.

Finally, by centering their campaign on opposition to the *extension* of slavery, the Republicans were able to keep the support of that great body of antislavery sentiment that had been nourished by the excitements of the past decade, while at the same time they attracted the support of those very considerable numbers of the population whose opposition to slavery extension was based upon economic grounds.

The answer to the problem of why the Republican party came to power is that it was due to a complex of causes. If pressed to single out the most important concrete factor, I would answer that it was the prospect of the extension of slavery. That prospect, and the excitements attendant upon it, had been of vital importance in keeping the party together and in augmenting the numbers of its adherents. But back of this lay certain idealistic and practical concepts. To those who voted the Republican ticket, the party represented Christian principles, democratic freedom, and economic progress—in other words, a moral and economic crusade.[39]

Whether economic or moral and idealistic opposition to slavery extension was the more important is a question that cannot be answered with certainty; but I am inclined to give greater weight to the moral and idealistic side. Lincoln put the case simply and clearly. "Slavery," he said in his Peoria speech of 1854, "is founded in the selfishness of man's nature—Opposition to it is (in?) his love of justice—Repeal the Missouri Compromise—repeal the Declaration of Independence—repeal all past history, you still can-

39 Craven, *Civil War in the Making,* 30–32.

not repeal human nature. It still will be the abundance of man's heart, that slavery extension is wrong; and out of the abundance of his heart his mouth will continue to speak." [40]

Years after the election was over, Carl Schurz wrote in his *Reminiscences:* "I think it can be said without exaggeration that there has never been in the history of this Republic a political movement in which moral motive was so strong,—indeed, so dominant and decisive." [41] It may not be altogether unhistorical to let that doughty old fighter in the fray have the last word.

40   Basler (ed.), *Collected Works of Abraham Lincoln,* II, 271.
41   Carl Schurz, *Reminiscences* (3 vols.; New York, 1907), II, 192.

Comment on

WHY THE REPUBLICAN PARTY CAME TO POWER

Don E. Fehrenbacher

My role as commentator fortunately does not require my engaging in a debate with Professor Van Deusen. It would be difficult to mount an extensive attack upon his lucid summary of the complex forces that brought the Republican party to power. There are, however, other ways of answering the question posed for this evening. I shall make an oblique approach to Professor Van Deusen's line of discussion, and in the process he may sustain a few nicks or scratches. Perhaps that will partially appease any persons in the audience who came expecting to see blood shed on the platform.

Our conference is not a full-scale inquiry into the causes of the Civil War, but rather an examination of that critical point where the causes began to produce their consequences. Nevertheless, before we are finished, every major aspect of Civil War causation will probably command our attention. One problem, and no doubt the preeminent one, concerns the centrality of slavery in the sectional conflict. Within the context of this evening's program, the question is whether the Republican party was primarily an antislavery organization. You will have noted that Professor Van Deusen, while giving much consideration to other factors, returns an affirmative answer.

Not long ago, in the heyday of Charles A. Beard, it was fashionable to regard the slavery controversy as a mask for economic revolution. Even the 1962 edition of Wilfred E. Binkley's *American*

Political Parties carries the statement that the slavery issue was "merely incidental" to the fundamental purpose of Republicanism and that the latter was "more a homestead than an antislavery party." But lately the trend of interpretation has been back toward the judgment of Abraham Lincoln, who said in 1858: "This slavery question has been the only one that has ever endangered our republican institutions." And in 1862: "Without slavery the rebellion could never have existed; without slavery it could not continue."

Yet even if it were generally agreed that slavery constituted the one essential element in the sectional conflict, the historian's work would be scarcely begun. For he must still trace the connections between slavery and war. He must explain why this particular issue, among all issues that have divided the American people, could not be settled within the framework of constitutional democracy. And here the problem is complicated by the fact that slavery meant so many different things and that it was attacked or defended for so many different reasons. There were Republicans, for example, who sympathized with the Negro and Republicans who detested the whole race. There were also Republicans like Lincoln, a humane man but not really a humanitarian, who viewed the subject on a more theoretical level, opposing slavery as a moral wrong and as a violation of the principles on which the nation had been founded. For others, slavery represented a roadblock in the way of economic progress; for others still, it was primarily an issue to be manipulated, cynically and ruthlessly, in a struggle for political power. Above all, the abstract word "slavery" connoted a series of concrete and inflammatory events, such as the various outbreaks of violence in Kansas, the Dred Scott decision, the Lecompton convention, and the martyrdom of John Brown. In the end, of course, nearly every item of public business became entangled with the slavery question.

The pattern is so complex that one is easily tempted to simplify matters by singling out some dominant feature. Professor Van Deusen, in summing up the Republican rise to power, lays special emphasis upon "the prospect of the extension of slavery." Yet that prospect had become exceedingly dim by the autumn of 1858. Thereafter, and perhaps all along, the territorial issue was but the skirmish line of a more extensive struggle. In his knowledge of subsequent events, Allan Nevins heavily stresses the "problem of race-adjustment" which loomed behind the problem of slavery. Yet it seems to me that his knowledge of subsequent events has in this case noticeably distorted Mr. Nevins' view of the 1850's. I doubt that we shall get any nearer to understanding the slavery controversy by stripping it like an artichoke in search of some ultimate core. Instead, we need to reconstruct an intricate configuration, then study carefully the relationship of part to part and part to whole. This is the only way to discover what we really mean by the assertion that slavery caused the Civil War.

A second question that almost invariably arises in any discussion of Civil War causation is whether the conflict was repressible or irrepressible. Here I enter a jungle so dark and confusing that I am impelled to make my first step a safe one by uttering an absurd truism. The Civil War, whatever it was a century ago, is now inevitable—or perhaps in this period of centennial enthusiasm I should say "unavoidable." Anyone who writes or reads the history of the 1850's will surely come in the end to Secession, Fort Sumter, and Bull Run. Not even in fiction, where Winston Churchill and MacKinlay Kantor have played with the idea of a Confederate victory, has any writer that I know of reshaped the past to the extent of eliminating the war entirely.

The irreversibility of history may seem too obvious to talk about, but we sometimes overlook its influence on historical explanation. The historian is expected not only to describe an event but to explain why it happened; and if he does his work thoroughly, as Professor Van Deusen has this evening, he is likely to leave the impression that it *had* to happen. "Always and everywhere," says Raymond Aron, ". . . there are discovered underlying and *valid* reasons which retrospectively confer an apparent necessity upon the effective outcome. It is forgotten that the opposite outcome might perhaps have permitted an equally satisfactory explanation. In other words, retrospection creates an *illusion of fatality* which contradicts the contemporary *impression of contingency*. Neither one is *a priori* true or false."

The historian, busy enough with his task of describing and explaining what actually happened, can seldom devote much time or space to presentation of the alternative possibilities that once existed. Yet he must be constantly aware of them; for one cannot evaluate what *did* happen without considering what *might* have happened. So there is nothing inherently foolish about asking whether a given historical occurrence was preventable. If nothing else, the question will serve as an antidote to the "illusion of fatality." The trouble with asking whether the Civil War was preventable is that the problem is just too big and too indefinite to be resolved by historical methods. The technique of retrospective prediction works best in dealing with specific events of limited duration. Historians concentrating upon the crisis of 1860–61 have a more manageable problem. Some of them, after viewing the missed opportunities and the narrow margins by which certain decisions were made, have not hesitated to declare that the war was indeed preventable at the time—that is, that it could have been at least postponed. And we of the 1960's can scarcely deny that prevention is often nothing more than a succession of postponements still in progress.

It may be that the forces tending to disrupt the Union were ultimately irresistible, but we can surely agree that the moment of decision would have come later if Lincoln had not been elected in 1860. Even then, only seven of the fifteen slave states seceded, and it is almost impossible to imagine a secession movement inspired by the election of Douglas, despite his unpopularity in the South. This evening, then, we may properly ask: Just how "irrepressible" was the Republican party in 1860?

Professor Van Deusen has already explained how the Republican organization emerged from a mass protest against the Kansas-Nebraska Act and established itself in 1856 as a major party, carrying eleven free states and winning 33 per cent of the popular vote. He adds, however, that the party was highly unstable and for a time "seemed doomed to a short and uneasy life." Elsewhere, I have suggested that "strong centrifugal tendencies in the political heritage and environment of the 1850's were highly conducive to the emergence of new combinations like the Republican party, but prejudicial to their subsequent growth and integration. Why Republicanism was born is perhaps a less important question than how it survived." By the latter part of 1858, slavery in the territories had ceased to be a pressing substantive issue. Seward had recently announced in the Senate that the battle was substantially won. Thus there was good reason to argue that the party had served its purpose, and that nothing more could be gained without endangering the Union. Yet in the election of 1860, Republicanism acquired a half million new adherents and captured the presidency. How shall we explain this second surge, which carried the party to victory?

Of course the Republicans, with their strength concentrated in the North, were able to win in the electoral college with only 40 per cent of the popular vote. It has sometimes been said that these results actually amounted to a rejection of Republicanism by the American people, and that Lincoln should have acted accordingly. Perhaps so, but in 1856 Buchanan had received only 45 per cent of the popular vote, and this had inspired no diffidence in Democratic ranks. The question, I suppose, is how small a winning plurality must be to constitute repudiation.

The Democrats, if we take the Northern and Southern wings together for a moment, likewise increased their percentage of the popular vote in 1860, but not in the right places. The biggest change occurred in the Whig-American organization, whose successor in 1860 was the Constitutional Union party. It was a change, furthermore, that took place only in the free states. The South in 1860 gave John Bell about the same support that it had given Millard Fillmore in 1856. But in the North, Bell salvaged merely 78,000 votes from the 395,000 cast for Fillmore. This sharp decline of 317,000 votes amounted to nearly 7 per cent of the national total—almost exactly the same as the Republican increase. It is not that simple, to be sure, for a considerable number of Know-Nothings evidently voted the Democratic ticket in 1860. Nevertheless, it seems clear that old-line Whigs and nativists contributed significantly to the Republican advance in some of the most critical states. Just why they did so remains to be answered.

One explanation is that the Republican party had taken a conservative turn by 1860, thereby winning the confidence of many moderate men. The rhetoric of the campaign and, to some extent, the party platform lend support to this view. At the same

time, however, the rise of new state leaders like John A. Andrew
of Massachusetts, Austin Blair of Michigan, and Oliver P. Morton
of Indiana might be offered as evidence of increasing radicalism.
My own opinion is that the conservative trend in the Republican
organization between 1856 and 1860 has been exaggerated. At
least it seems equally justifiable to say that many conservatives,
aroused at last by events of the period, veered toward Republicanism. One thing is certainly clear. The party's alleged change
of pace or change of direction made no impression on the South.

The Republicans, to be sure, did display soberer judgment in
selecting their presidential candidate for 1860. In every respect
except political stature, Lincoln was the ideal choice, and the
recent example of Franklin Pierce suggested that obscurity might
not be altogether a handicap. The nomination of Lincoln may
have been decisive in states like Illinois and Indiana, where
Seward was widely considered not only too radical on the slavery
question but too forthright in his opposition to nativism.

Another explanation of the Republican victory is that the party
broadened its appeal to economic interests. Homesteads, internal
improvements, and the tariff unquestionably received much attention in the campaign; and one must, I suppose, concede some
correlation between how politicians talk and how people vote.
Yet in view of the low value ordinarily placed upon party platforms, it is a little surprising that historians should attach so
much importance to the Republican platform of 1860.

Leaving the tariff question for consideration in a different context, let us look for a moment at the supposed influence of the
homestead plank upon the election in the Northwest. Even
Professor Van Deusen, who can hardly be accused of overstress-
ing economic factors, declares: "That Lincoln received 54 per
cent of the total vote of Iowa, 56 per cent in Wisconsin, 57 per
cent in Michigan, and 60 per cent in Minnesota was in considerable part due to the land issue." But does he mean that the promise of homesteads actually carried those states for the Republicans,
or that it merely enlarged their majorities? Back in 1856, when
there was no homestead plank in the platform, Iowa, Wisconsin,
and Michigan had all given their electoral votes to Frémont
(Minnesota did not enter the Union until 1858). Are we to be-

lieve that a Democratic resurgence in the Northwest was fore-stalled by the homestead appeal of 1860? There is little evidence to support such a contention. Furthermore, if the hope of obtaining free land was so decisive on the frontier, one wonders why nearly two-thirds of the voters in California and Oregon remained loyal Democrats. The purpose of these observations is not to deny the widespread interest in the homestead idea, but rather to challenge some of the sweeping and unverifiable claims made for it. To me, the facts suggest that the issue generally tended to strengthen the resolve of voters already committed to Republicanism for other reasons.

It is also possible to explain any victory by detailing the weaknesses of the losing side. "There persists," says Binkley, "an almost ineradicable delusion that Lincoln slipped into office because the Democratic vote was split." But even if the opposition had concentrated its 60 per cent of the popular vote on one candidate, the Republicans would have emerged with a majority in the electoral college. It can be argued, of course, that a united and more confident Democratic party would have made a better showing. On the other hand, as Professor Van Deusen has pointed out, a candidate fully supported by the slaveholding South might have lost votes in the critical free states. The burden of proof seems to rest upon those whose retrospective prediction substantially alters the cold election figures.

Finally, one can interpret the election of 1860 by examining the pivotal free states which were carried by Buchanan in 1856 and by Lincoln four years later. The three most important of these were Pennsylvania, Indiana, and Illinois. Here the historian discovers some striking contrasts that discourage easy generalizations and bespeak the importance of timing and locality. In Illinois, 91 counties were carried by the same party in 1856 and 1860. Only four counties shifted from the Democratic to the Republican column. In Indiana, 66 counties repeated themselves, and 25 changed from Democratic to Republican. In Pennsylvania, 28 counties repeated, and 35 changed from Democratic to Republican. The Democrats won in only twelve Pennsylvania counties, and their statewide popular vote actually declined by 35,000, while the Republican total increased by 120,000.

It seems clear that Illinois Republicanism reached almost its full strength as early as 1856. Indeed, the party captured the state administration in that year and lost the presidential contest only because of the Fillmore diversion. In 1858 a narrow Republican majority was offset by a minor inequity in the apportionment of legislative seats, which enabled Douglas to defeat Lincoln. The election of 1860 was also very close in the state. Thus the relative strength of the two parties changed only slightly in Illinois between 1856 and 1860. The change was greater in Indiana and greatest of all in Pennsylvania, which, more than any other state of the Union, underwent a political revolution during those years. Why did Republicanism not only survive but flourish after 1856? Pennsylvania, since it came so late and yet so emphatically into the Republican camp, should provide some significant clues.

First, let it be said that what happened in Pennsylvania can be explained in several ways. There was, for example, the virtual bankruptcy of Democratic leadership, in sharp contrast with Illinois. Historians, however, have usually stressed economic factors. Specifically, the Panic of 1857 caused much distress in Pennsylvania and inspired loud demands for higher tariffs to protect domestic producers from foreign competition. No one will deny that protection received abundant notice in the Pennsylvania campaign of 1860, or that the Republicans, both in their national platform and on the floor of Congress, had conspicuously supported tariff revision. But how many votes did the party manufacture with this issue? Enough to account for a majority of more than 70,000?

Tariff or no tariff, many financiers and industrialists feared the economic effects of a Lincoln victory and gave their support to other candidates. Not even an ardent protectionist necessarily placed higher duties first on his list of priorities. But let us look more closely at the problem of numbers. The most persistent tariff men were probably the iron manufacturers, and Pennsylvania, more than one historian tells us, made half of the country's iron. The census of 1860 reveals, however, that there were 251 iron-founders in Pennsylvania, 235 ironmongers, and not quite 4,000 ironworkers. On the other hand, I find that there were 15,000 blacksmiths, whose interest in higher iron prices must have been less than enthusiastic. And glancing down through the whole list of three or four hundred occupations, from the 180,000 farmers and 30,000 carpenters to the 11 ventriloquists and 5 trussmakers, one wonders just how many voters were converted to Republicanism by the promise of prosperity through manipulation of import duties.

Moreover, with a little further investigation, we find that the political revolution in Pennsylvania was largely accomplished before the Republicans formally embraced the tariff and made it a lively issue. The elections of 1858 amounted to a Democratic disaster in the free states and especially in Pennsylvania. There the party lost not only the statehouse but eleven of its fifteen seats in Congress. So the Republicans first captured Pennsylvania in the immediate aftermath of the bitter controversy over the Lecompton constitution. Their triumph was primarily a stern rebuke to an administration that had tried to force the admission of Kansas as a slave state. The Lecompton struggle, which split the Democratic party, also cost that party its last footholds in the North. It may be that the most important single decision of the 1850's was Buchanan's decision to endorse the work of the Lecompton convention. From that point on, the odds were plainly with the Republicans.

This emphasis upon the Lecompton controversy is but another way of saying again that the Republican party was essentially an antislavery party. It likewise reinforces my suggestion that the Republican movement was above all a series of responses to concrete events. Not only the great issue of the time but the terrible weight of what had been done and what had been *said* pressed heavily upon Americans in 1860.

II

WHY THE DEMOCRATIC PARTY DIVIDED

Roy F. Nichols

Like the causes of the Civil War, the reasons for the disintegration of the Democratic party in 1860 can be and have been elaborated at any desired length. Rather than repeat the varieties of exegesis involved in the use of such terms as the morals of slavery, the economic rivalry of diverse interests, the cultural conflict between the sections, and the ecological and demographic elements among the determinants, it is more realistic to consider some concepts in group dynamics, in the behavior of individuals, small groups, and the masses in political association. For the crux of the matter lay in the fact that complex party machinery collapsed in a context of human failure. Because the behavior involved in failure depends on the nature of the stimulation created by individuals and groups through the senses of sight and hearing for those others in association, an analysis of it becomes a study in communication. In other words, the analysis involves a consideration of who meets whom, of what is said and seen during the course of recurrent interchanges, and, what is less obvious and therefore harder to discover, the kind of reaction countless nervous systems produce when confronted with the presence and behavior of other organisms.

An understanding of such complexity requires a close look at the series of meetings which brought into one train of communication the political operators who directed the Democratic party's conventions in several large meeting halls and in auxiliary places of accommodation. Here was generated the great and devastating explosion of human emotion which in time rocked the growing nation to its foundations, for the national conventions of the Democratic party were significant bridges of communication over which the "great forces" moved to influence the behavior of the nation's political operators.

In Charleston, Richmond, Washington, and Baltimore in April, May, and June of 1860, there were a concentration and dispersion of definable and identifiable human beings through which the forces shaping political behavior operated. It was there that the doctrinaire position of certain Southern Democrats insisting on an endorsement of an impossible idea encountered the overweening ambitions of Douglas and his followers who were determined to maintain power by demanding a heroic bit of realism. Such a collision produced a fatal impasse. In the almost unbelievable confusion of these meetings it was demonstrated that the Democratic party after thirty years of success was not strong enough, despite its age, its experience, and the skill of its operators, to maintain itself midst the confusion into which the action and interaction of the numerous forces shaping this growing nation had plunged American politics.

The ingenious men who created the republic of the United States of America were remarkably successful after the Revolution in performing their huge task. But in one particular their achievement was less than perfect: this was in the matter of the creation of the executive branch. If they were to have one at all, and there was some doubt that they should, and if they were to avoid a monarch, they were required to invent something for which there were few, if any, helpful precedents. They wanted the executive to be equal and coordinate with the legislative and the judicial arms; therefore they refused to let it be chosen by Congress. The sprawling population without any adequate system of communication could not be trusted to go to the polls and vote for an individual choice. The names would be so numerous that consensus would appear impossible. The result was the creation of a college of electors to be appointed by such means as each state might prescribe. These men were to have this choice as their sole responsibility. The founding fathers gave no directions to the states save specifying the exact number of electors, that their choice should be over thirty-five years of age, and that there should be a reassignment of executive power made possible every four years. Each leap year the complicated mechanism of choice would operate to enable the voters to make a change; the inexorable regularity of this choice despite current conditions was a fateful prescription.

There proved to be a good deal of uncertainty about how to operate this machinery of selection. At first it seemed amazingly simple, no problem at all. Every elector without any known concert turned to the great leader George Washington. He served for two terms by unanimous consent and could probably have continued, so revered a symbol of popular faith and security had he become. But after eight years he sought in effect to turn his office over to the Vice-President, John Adams. Here unity ceased. The new republic was divided by geography, and the resulting cleavage showed up clearly in 1796. A bloc of electors, predominantly Southern, voted for Thomas Jefferson of Virginia rather than for the Massachusetts Adams; and instead of having a Virginia President and a Massachusetts Vice-President, there was to be a Massachusetts President and a Virginia Vice-President, this same Jefferson, but by a narrow margin of three votes.

The world confusion resulting from the French Revolution and the ensuing world war involved the new republic in an internal contest between those who loved liberty and those who feared centralization. These divisions involved contests over the control of the executive branch, and the Congress undertook to designate the presidental candidates to be pitted one against the other. The Virginians and the New Yorkers at the capital city developed a sort of an alliance which New England and South Carolina undertook to combat. This division and these contests in a society so large and geographically diversified soon showed the need of a new institutional construct. As nobody ever very explicitly realized what was lacking nor ever at any given time glimpsed what the remedy should be, no one ever set up a commission or a conference to define the need or propose its remedy. Yet a solution of sorts emerged in the shape of a fourth branch of government. To the specified executive, legislative, and judicial arms there was added a federal system of parties without constitutional or even legal warrant. Much unbudgeted time was spent without system or designated period in constructing this fourth branch. Its creation was marked by much trial and error; and one of its failures, that suffered by the Democratic party in 1860, was spectacular.

Party organization as such began first in the states. It was of slow growth on the national scene because after 1800 popular interest in presidential contests became usually perfunctory. The truth was that the presidency was not particularly important, and outside of Virginia not many were interested in such a caretaking job. A sort of factional palace guard politics in the White House and Capitol sufficed; a congressional caucus passed the presidency from Jefferson to Madison to Monroe, all Virginians. Few seemed to care who was President—a situation difficult to understand today.

In the 1820's a new political era dawned, and the republic started over again the study of how to choose a President. A new set of conditions determined the process. The nation was much larger in area; its population had increased; people had been moving westward; the original thirteen states were now twenty-four. Various interests in the growing society felt the need of more facilities for manufacturing, transportation, and finance and in such measure as the states individually could not supply. There must be central mobilization and direction. The presidency was becoming a prize to be sought. So the original mechanism, slightly modified by the twelfth amendment, now got new usage.

In 1824 the election device worked as the founders had planned it. The electors made nominations, and from the list, Congress chose. But the process proved most cumbrous and hard to operate; worse, it invited all sorts of negotiation and intrigue which many thought made a mockery of popular government. The confusion and uncertainty of 1824–25 could not be tolerated very often. Certain of those who had succeeded in organizing political machinery on the state plane believed that the answer was to extend their systems to the national level.

In a double decade of effort some of these ambitious state leaders, expert organizers, and resourceful presidential candidates undertook to create two national political organizations which every four years would organize the contest for the presidency. The first of these to emerge was the Jacksonian phalanx. These operators seized upon the "Corrupt Bargain" of 1824 which had deprived the Hero of New Orleans of the prize and by clever use of all their talents and opportunities created a party. These partisans mobilized a hurrahing force to elect Old Hickory and defeat the corrupt union of the blackleg and the puritan, Henry Clay and John Quincy Adams, who had stolen victory from their hero in 1825. The election of 1828 was the first of the contests in which popular enthusiasm was invoked to rally voters to a standard rather than to a platform. It was not the last, but fortunately it was not to establish a pattern consistently followed.

When Jackson was installed, the insiders saw him as an old, sick, and sorrowing man who would scarcely last out his term and would certainly not be in the running for 1832. So who was to succeed him? It looked to many as though the contest would be between the Vice-President, John C. Calhoun, and the Secretary of State, Henry Clay. Calhoun, a pure Republican of 1798–99 who had repented of his centralizing heresies and was ready to reform the Republican party, seemed destined for great things. Clay on his part was espousing a centralizing American system, and others had their hopes of thus repeating the difficulties of 1824–25. But this was not to be.

Two well-organized state machines had plans of their own. Virginia and New York, who off and on had been working together since 1791, now came to a new understanding. The Richmond Junto and the Albany Regency were joining forces. The leader of the regency, Martin Van Buren, with his flair for organization soon concluded that Calhoun was too doctrinaire, too inflexible, and too uncomprehending of practical politics to have the flexibility needed for meeting the needs of the swiftly growing nation; also the two were temperamentally incompatible, and their personal ambitions clashed. Van Buren cleverly insinuated himself into Jackson's good graces and cut down his rival. Then he cemented the understanding with the Richmond Junto and Thomas Ritchie, its editor and propaganda scribe. An idea of Ritchie's was adopted and a national convention worked up by Jackson's kitchen cabinet, Van Buren and Francis P. Blair, after Jackson had been persuaded to run for a second term.

Conventions had been a device concocted by the English when

they wanted something unusual or unprecedented done in politics. A group of professionals would get together in force; and, speaking for the realm, they would indicate some action, notably recalling the Stuarts to the throne. The convention idea had traveled across the seas and was a potent instrument in the American Revolution. Colonial conventions, or Congresses as they were called, and particularly the Continental Congresses and the Constitutional Convention of 1787, were in effect party conventions designed to mobilize supporters for an idea. Now in the 1830's the device was to be used again. The caucus system had proved unsatisfactory. It had fallen out of repute and the factions lacked mobilization. The growing state organizations increasingly were not interested in congressional direction. The Anti-Masons and the National Republicans resorted to the convention device in 1830 and 1831, and the followers of Jackson took it up in 1832. Their main purpose was to eliminate Calhoun, with whom Jackson was feuding, and to substitute Van Buren for Vice-President; they undertook to use a convention as their instrument for this purpose. They would call the "professionals" from the several states to Baltimore where they would have a "briefing" session and secure agreement that Van Buren should be the candidate for Vice-President. Such a gathering, in a sense a "trade" organization of the professionals, would insure communication with Jacksonians in all the states, regardless of whether they had any Congressmen.

This convention was cannily designed to aid the "central direction" of the professionals in presenting a united front against their organized opponents and at the same time in keeping their internal factions as nearly impotent as possible. They knew Jackson's support was not universal. He could not expect to carry a number of states, perhaps in the neighborhood of 40 per cent. These blank spots were, in a sense, "rotten boroughs." The professionals wanted representation from them present who were to go home filled with the spirit to conduct missionary work for Jackson, but they did not want them in a position to control events. So the managers instituted the two-thirds rule designed to prevent unruly factions from doing business with these representatives of areas where there was no Jackson strength and to prevent them from gaining control by securing a bare majority of convention votes. The managers wanted to be sure that despite accidents they would have at least a veto which they could use to force a consensus. They anticipated no situation in which they could not control at least one-third of the convention membership.

Under these circumstances the Jacksonian professionals from the several states inaugurated the practice of coming together every four years on the eve of presidential elections to perfect their strength and organization. From 1832 until 1856 they met in Baltimore. These bodies grew in size with the nation and at the same rate as Congress. The problems which they considered varied with the particular gathering. In 1832 such a meeting had eliminated Calhoun and had ratified Jackson's choice of Van Buren as his Vice-President. In 1836 it was necessary to find a dynamic candidate for Vice-President of heroic mold and Western appeal to augment the presidential candidacy of the colorless, Eastern Van Buren. In 1840, as Calhoun had returned to the fold after a brief sojourn with the Whigs, an agreement on the terms of political reunion had to be negotiated, and the Democrats' first platform was presented.

For a decade these Democratic national conventions functioned with a reasonable degree of efficiency. But the next ten years told another story. Calhoun's presidential ambitions were not finally completely frustrated in the 1840's and he turned his bitterness on the convention which he charged was an instrument of the spoilsmen. Upon their manipulations he blamed much of his discomfiture. He and his followers wanted to change its rules and upon occasion refused to attend its sessions. Also a new generation, tired of Van Buren and the domination of his henchmen, demanded a "new deal." They were dismayed by the defeat of 1840 and by the rising Whigs; they feared Henry Clay might beat the rather shopworn "Little Van" in 1844. A group of Southern and Western politicos with some help from New England took over the convention in 1844 from the traditional Van Buren managers; the nomination of a "dark horse" was negotiated in the person of James Knox Polk.

Polk's selection was a convention maneuver engineered by a combination of state and congressional managers which eventually was to result in the disruption and disaffection of the New York party. This split in large part occurred because Polk developed no aptitude for party leadership. He was an avowed one-term candidate and thereby abdicated as party leader as soon as he had distributed the patronage. His efforts to heal the breach within New York by distributing offices was a dismal failure; and his foreign policy in Mexico and Oregon, despite its spectacular success, served to break up the New York party for years to come.

This schism destroyed the unity of the leaderless national convention of 1848. Here for the first time a candidate from the Northwest, General Lewis Cass, received the nomination; but the Van Buren half of the New Yorkers walked out because they were not recognized as *the* Democracy and later joined with certain antislavery groups in forming an enlarged Free-Soil party. This break rather unfairly got the credit for the party's defeat in the fall at the hands of the hero, General Zachary Taylor. The precedent of walking out of a national convention had been set, and the secessionists were given credit for a capacity to defeat which they probably did not deserve.

In the conventions of 1844 and 1848 a new device was being set up for control: the National Committee presumed to give direction to the management of the party conclaves. However, by 1852 it had not achieved full stature; and, in the wake of the defeat of 1848, the party seemed to be drifting, for a second time leaderless, toward 1852. The professionals, by and large attracted by the understandings of 1848 and their status which had been established in that campaign, seemed inclined to renominate Cass now that the schism of 1848 apparently had been healed by a tenuous reunion of the wings of the New York party and by the Compromise of 1850. But such a variety of contestants arose opposing following this ancient trail that confusion began to descend.

The convention of 1852 promised to be a symbol of impotence. It was at this junction that a self-appointed inner group emerged to take over. One of Cass's chief rivals was James Buchanan of Pennsylvania, a candidate since 1844. His Pennsylvania managers joined a Southern bloc from Virginia, North Carolina, Georgia, Alabama, and Mississippi, some of whom had been active in the 1844 coup, to produce another dark horse. A combination of

New Englanders and Mexican War generals from the Aztec Club had been pushing as second choice a New Hampshire brigadier general, Franklin Pierce; and he was the one the cabal "put over." They completed the ticket with Buchanan's friend, Senator William R. King of Alabama. The nonentity of this ticket, plus the pacifying influence of the Compromise of 1850 and the absurdity of General Winfield Scott as an opposing candidate, made Pierce's electoral college majority huge although his majority of the popular vote was slim.

Pierce had even less capacity for party leadership than had Polk, and despite his deceptive victory in 1852 the party was soon in difficulties. The New England President not only made similar mistakes in handling party patronage but he had none of Polk's success in foreign policy and in congressional legislation. Most unfortunately he joined Douglas and other Senators in engineering the castastrophic repeal of the Missouri Compromise, and almost immediately a precocious phoenix arose from the ashes of the Whig party in the form of the young Republican eagle, dedicated to furthering Northern interests. The congressional elections of 1854–55 sounded a sharp warning which at first no one seemed able to heed. Were the days of Democratic power and Southern security numbered?

The maneuverings anticipating the Democratic convention of 1860 really began in 1856. As that fateful presidential year approached, the Democrats found themselves face to face for the first time with their new foe of unknown potential, the Republican party, born in an atmosphere of moral indignation and promotional expectation. Under these circumstances they commenced another chapter in their history. During their first decade they had been led by an efficient group of Jacksonian operators, Van Buren and his Albany Regency and the Richmond Junto associates; and at first Francis P. Blair, Sr., was in charge of the propaganda. In the 1840's the management was seized by a younger group with some senatorial guidance including lower South, Southwestern and Western participation and with old Father Ritchie taking over Blair's pen.

This guidance during the second phase had produced three candidates, Polk, Cass, and Pierce, two of them dark horses and the latter two not fortunate in their leadership. None of these candidates had been of Jacksonian stature. Despite the disasters during the Pierce regime and the threat of the new Republicans, this inept management seemed about to give Pierce the usually available renomination with the blessing of almost the solid South, the popular sovereignty West, and New England Democrats who were emotionally committed to their "first success." Such an invitation to defeat appeared so disturbing that it invited new leadership.

On the eve of the convention of 1856 a few practical operators came to the conclusion that they must intervene. A self-appointed senatorial group therefore decided to try a coup something along the order of the one of 1844. It is significant of the nature of the system of party control that the move originated in the Senate. Four Senators, John Slidell and Judah P. Benjamin of Louisiana, J. D. Bright of Indiana, and James A. Bayard of Delaware, motivated not only by a determination to avert defeat but also by extreme dislike of Douglas and a combination of distrust and contempt for Pierce, set up a headquarters at the convention in the house of a railroad promoter in Cincinnati, a new location for the national conventions. The Democratic National Committee headed by a Maryland chairman had decided that perhaps they had met in Baltimore long enough and that the growth of the Western wing of the party demanded recognition. Therefore they had picked out Cincinnati, the Queen City of the West, for the point of congregation; and it was thither that the Senatorial cabal wended its way.

Its members planned to accomplish their purpose by throwing overboard Pierce, bypassing Douglas, and negotiating the nomination of the veteran James Buchanan. His great assets were his long career and expert knowledge, the fact that he had been out of the country since 1853 and thus had avoided the Kansas malaise, and finally the fact that the hardheaded Senator Slidell of Louisiana thought of him as "his man." These contrivers succeeded. They formed a scattered combination led by Pennsylvania, Virginia, and Louisiana which could and did stop Pierce and Douglas and named Old Buck.

But the nomination of Buchanan was not all that happened at

Cincinnati. When the Pierce cause became hopeless his strength was transferred to Douglas. Despite the shift Buchanan soon secured a majority; and at this point instead of fighting it out further and perhaps forcing another dark horse in at the finish, Douglas retired gracefully. Whether to secure this he had been promised a clear field in 1860 or whether he merely hoped he would have it because of his action is anybody's guess. Probably Douglas took encouragement from his situation. At any rate his friend John C. Breckinridge of Kentucky was nominated for the vice-presidency. The disappointed Southern supporters of Pierce would be somewhat placated, it was hoped, by designating Charleston, South Carolina, as the place for the Convention of 1860.

The administration of James Buchanan, the veteran expert, was even more disastrous than that of the novice, Pierce. The new President suffered every disaster from dysentery to John Brown's raid. Douglas likewise had had a trying four years. Buchanan slighted him in distributing patronage. The Supreme Court declared popular sovereignty, his great principle upon which he depended to harmonize Northern and Southern support, to be unconstitutional. The practical working of this provision had blown up in Kansas and had placed him in an almost unbearable dilemma in Congress. He had beaten Lincoln, but he had been compelled to advertise his rival's political skill. His Southern colleagues had taken away his chairmanship of the Senate Committee on Territories, thus depriving him even of office space. His wife had lost their baby through a miscarriage, and he himself had been seriously ill. Despite all this he had been picking up delegates and endorsements.

The climax of calamity came in the form of John Brown's raid in October, 1859, almost on the eve of the Charleston Convention. This disaster set the stage for a third coup, and for a third time its chief operators were in the Senate. When the Congress came together in December, 1859, Brown had just been hanged, certain elements in the South were arming and drilling, and there was no party in certain control of the House though it seemed likely that the Republicans would take over. The Republican management was preparing campaign literature for 1860 which was interpreted as endorsing the idea of slave uprising, and Douglas had appealed from the Supreme Court to history and had published a magazine article proving by historical evidence that the South was without any platform. Also the census of 1860 was being projected, and its figures quite obviously would register the fact that the South was doomed politically to hopeless minority. To the Southern Democracy the prospect was desperate, and to make it unbearable Douglas was the only candidate of prominence. In fact he might easily come to Charleston with a majority of the votes, certainly enough to stop anybody else under the two-thirds rule and to secure an endorsement of the popular sovereignty platform of 1856.

While the House took another frightening two months to organize, thus repeating 1855, the wheels of government were stalled. The Senate had time on its hands and a Southern bloc, reminiscent of those of 1844 and 1856, planned again. What they did has been called a "conspiracy"—this is a somewhat hysterical term, but it is near enough the truth to warrant its use in quotation marks. Certain Senators, and here we find Slidell and his Cincinnati associates working together with Jefferson Davis and a group of other Southern solons, had arrived at a determination. Apprehension had reached such a pitch in their constituencies that their Whig-American opponents were preparing to be 100 per cent Southern and fight them on the ground that they were "soft" on squatter sovereignty which was selling the South down the river. They must have an explicit endorsement of Southern rights in the Charleston platform. Jefferson Davis, in assuming Calhoun's mantle, wrote the formula which was presented to the Senate the day the Republicans at long last organized the House. If this platform was not accepted, the South would leave the convention as the Barnburners had in 1848. As an earnest of this the Alabama state Democratic convention instructed its delegation to Charleston to take the lead in this walkout if the demand was refused.

How far the senatorial managers had gone toward making a firm decision on breaking up the convention at this time is not of record. The indications are that they had, for it should be remembered that there was a code of honor observed in certain Southern political quarters under which it was dishonorable for delegates to refuse to support the program prescribed by a convention in which they had participated. There was a possibility that the Southern platform might be defeated and Douglas nominated. As a significant number of Southern delegates had determined never to support Douglas on a squatter sovereignty platform, honor bound them if they were defeated on platform to leave before he or anyone was nominated on a platform they could not accept.

A further step was also under discussion. What should be done if a Republican were elected in 1860? Here again Alabama serves as an indicator. Her state legislature passed a law requiring her governor, in that event, to summon a state convention to determine whether Alabama should secede. The question of the formation of a confederacy was likewise discussed. How far definite plans were formulated again cannot be categorically stated. It was an age of romantic empiricism so beefed up by hyperbolic rhetoric that it is difficult to discover exactly what some of these extravagant speakers were thinking. Despite the variety of possibilities talked about, it is probable that only one firm decision had been reached. There must be an "honest platform," or the party must be judged to have outlived its usefulness and be scrapped. Such action would clear the stage for new political engineering. Congress might take over. There might be a new Constitutional Convention as Calhoun had proposed. There might be secession and the formation of a new confederacy.

Douglas was living in the midst of this planning and sharing in some of its convivial moments. The practical Eastern operators were fully aware of what was going on; and at least one Republican Senator, William H. Seward, who most observers thought might well be that party's nominee in 1860, was on intimate terms with certain of his Senatorial colleagues from the South. It must not be forgotten that the Senate was a species of social club.

With some general lines of strategy laid out, Slidell, Bright, and Bayard went to Charleston and set up headquarters at the convention city, this time behind an ice cream saloon. From the moment of the opening of the convention shock tactics were employed, an old convention technique. Douglas' strength must be discovered at once and his managers, who after all came in large part from rotten boroughs or from states which could not deliver an electoral vote, must be given unmistakable warning that if the convention didn't damn well take the Southern platform, Douglas and the party could go to hell. This notice was registered in no uncertain terms by shouting, by climbing on tables, by variegated parliamentary disorder, and by threats and certain forms of alcoholic exaggeration.

The Douglas forces were ill-prepared for such a shock. They had come down into this atmosphere, new and strange to them, under close organization and strict discipline. They had hired a hall and set up a dormitory in it where they all slept row on row and where their leaders could keep track of them. They were probably very uncomfortable in the unaccustomed heat and also conscious of their lack of status in aristocratic Charleston. Politically they were as desperate as the Southerners. If they went home with this "honest" platform of Southern rights how could they survive in even the few Northern states left to them after the near disaster of 1856? Douglas was their only chance with some platform that had at least a coincidental resemblance to squatter sovereignty, Douglas' "great brinziple" of "let the people rule." Only this could beat "no more slave states" and "let freedom ring."

But it must not be forgotten that there was a third element in the compound. New York was back in strength though with the usual contest on hand. New York's truculent mayor, Fernando Wood, had tried to capture the management of the party in New York state by strong-arm methods at the state convention. He was in Charleston working up Southern support for his contesting delegation on the ground that his New York City was the only Democratic stronghold left in New York and that he and his "shoulder-hitters," as they were called, were the only outfit which could deliver. Pennsylvania, New Jersey, and the New England states were there likewise looking for the main chance. They had no particular loyalty to Douglas though they recognized his vote-getting power. Their main interest was a negotiated peace; they wanted somehow to trade it out by prestidigious manipulations of words and candidates.

All factions were confronted by statistics. The Southern states had only 120 electoral votes. The victor in the electoral college needed 152. The required 32 votes must come from free states. Southern statisticians figured however that these 32 could probably be acquired only at a semantic price which might cost 34 votes in those Southern states that could go Whig. What a dilemma and besides the weather was hot, the hotels were expensive, bad, and hellishly crowded, and the meeting hall was atrocious. Calhoun's bones rested in a neighboring church yard; perhaps his spirit hovered disapprovingly over the convention which he had always distrusted.

Thirty years of convention experience were drawn upon to discover the way out of this statistical and emotional confusion. The Southerners, who had on occasion shared Calhoun's dislike for conventions, served their violent notice. The Douglasites with their numerical majority sought to change it into a two-thirds endorsement by controlling the committees and the crucial floor votes. The "practical operators" sought to arrange accommodations. But the forces would not budge.

When the Douglas platform, though somewhat modified, was adopted, Alabama began the projected walkout. However the exit was disappointing, only eight of the fifteen slave states responded; and these were only from the lower South. The seceders, despite their disappointment, settled down in an adjacent hall. One of the objects of this secession was to establish possible negotiations which might bring about a compromise nomination or a revised platform or both. Some of the seceders thought that under such circumstances they might still go home not only with a good chance of keeping their local strength but also with some hope of national victory. They would bet on enough support from Northerners who feared Seward's higher law and irrepressible conflict heresies to get the Northern votes necessary. They counted on Seward's enemies within his own party and the distrust of his radicalism in his own section. Let it be remembered that nobody in Charleston then dreamed of Lincoln. Also some of the leading Senators were boon companions of Seward and would have suffered him, not gladly perhaps, but as an alternative to Douglas whose guts they hated. But not only were they not joined by the majority of the South, no one even came to offer overtures for reunion. It was an anticlimax just to sit, despite the fact that they were cheered by the inability of those they called "the rump" to accomplish anything.

The only positive step achieved was the fact that a numerical majority cast their votes for Douglas. The Douglas managers had expected that when the Southerners seceded, two-thirds of the remaining quorum were all that would be necessary to nominate. This was one reason why some of them were in effect anxious to get at least a few of the Southern delegates out. But New York defeated this, holding the door open even wider for negotiation. It would have taken more skill and concession to secure 202 than 168, but since Douglas seemed able to muster only 152½, he would have to make concessions to those who were adept at manipulation.

After balloting fifty-seven times the convention decided on an unprecedented act. On the morning of the tenth day the members recessed until June 18, then to reassemble in Baltimore. Both factions would go home to sound out opinion. The Douglasites hoped that others could be found in the seceders' districts to repudiate them and less intransigent Democrats to fill their places in Baltimore. The seceders could but hope for the endorsement of their stand.

During the ensuing six weeks the hopes of the Douglas managers were in part fulfilled. New delegations were dispatched from Alabama, Arkansas, Georgia, and Louisiana. The original delegates from Mississippi and Texas returned. Those from Florida were in the city but did not attend the sessions as delegates. The controlling facts were probably certain events in the weeks between the two conventions. The Whigs and Americans together with other conservatives had organized a new party called the Constitutional Union party and had nominated John Bell of Tennessee and Edward Everett of Massachusetts on a simple platform endorsing the Constitution and the Union. This ticket would be likely to be strong in the South. Then, too, Abraham Lincoln, not Seward, had been nominated by the Republicans upon a platform offering generous subsidies. Lincoln's slate would be more formidable than any headed by Seward. Facing such developments the Southern wing felt it impossible to yield on their platform, and the Northern wing on their candidate.

Thus the experienced politicos, who had faced walkouts before and had composed differences on several occasions, and their less tutored associates found themselves without any of the familiar materials with which to work: neither faction would advance concessions on either principles or candidates. An unprecedented impasse had been reached, and no accommodation was achieved. The majority nominated Douglas as they had determined to do from the beginning while the traders from the middle states sat by helpless and of necessity acquiescent. The seceders, joined by the rest of the South and a few from Northern constituencies, chose the Vice-President, John C. Breckinridge, and a Senator, Joseph Lane of Oregon, to head the ticket on the "honest platform." This was canny. Now that there were four tickets, the contest might be thrown into Congress. The likelihood that the splintered House could muster a majority of the states for any of those who might be the three highest seemed remote. But the safely Democratic Senate would have no difficulty in choosing their colleague, Joseph Lane. The Democrats might thus save the presidency after all. Some perhaps looked ahead to another contingency. If there were to be secession, it could be convenient to have the Vice-President of the United States, Breckinridge, in a position to help in their effort. But to most it looked as if the Democrats had elected Lincoln.

Thus the Democratic party broke up when its national convention collapsed in 1860. A bloc of Southern delegates shattered the organization deliberately. They had come to Charleston with no candidate to propose. In the convention they made much of formulae. Though the majority of the delegates were against them, they sought to control because they had a majority of the states. As they demanded full recognition of the rights of the states, they proclaimed themselves firm supporters of the Constitution which they maintained was more important than the Union. They had been suffering in power and prestige ever since 1856. Then they had failed to renominate Pierce. Twice they had lost control of the House of Representatives. Now in 1860 they had lost control of the national convention. Power meant a great deal to them as it naturally would in an aggregation in which so many were slaveholders. Particularly after the shock of John Brown's raid, power was more than ever necessary for protection and survival. They must have the autonomy with security which Calhoun had prescribed. If they could not find it in the old Union, they would create a new agency to insure it.

So they would destroy the convention and the party as instruments no longer serving their purpose. They were ready to try something new. Douglas and his associates on their part strove desperately to salvage the party mechanism. But they were not strong enough; and besides, they had nothing to take its place. The convention system latterly had been plagued by a weakness which was now proving fatal. The professionals who had invented and operated it had failed to provide real leadership. They had preferred usually to nominate their own kind. They were not favorable to superior talent, to statesmen, or to the nineteenth century equivalent of "eggheads." They chose those who spoke their language and understood their own mores. The Democrats had never in these years of convention practice nominated a man of great talent or commanding reputation. One can go far without finding a more colorless group than Van Buren, Polk, Cass, Pierce, or Buchanan. They were certainly not much more than representatives of the average man. Van Buren and Buchanan were men of experience and craft but with no capacity to deal with the unusual. Polk had some skill and luck, but he was a man of decided limitations, a statesman incapable of foreseeing or forestalling dangers; even less can be said for Cass and Pierce.

The nation was growing fast in size, wealth, and power. It was also fragmentizing, falling apart because of its own weight. Emotions were getting out of hand, morals were deteriorating, health was bad, and the nature of republican self-government was yielding to temptation and succumbing to corruption. But the leadership necessary to recall men to their duty in maintaining the ideals of democracy could not be summoned by any of the instruments available.

It cannot be said with certainty that in 1860 and in the preceding years a consistently higher grade of leadership would have solved more of the problems and avoided more of the crises, but it can be emphasized that no leadership which could cope with the troubled times became available. Rather the current methods required the choosing of those who patently could not rouse the innate capacities of the people of the United States. A party requires leadership to be effective; one cannot carry any society through trying times by a committee or a conference. There must be a personality, a symbol which can inspire trust and confidence, a personality whom the mass will follow.

It can never be known what might have happened had the Convention of 1860 been able to agree on a platform and on a candidate. With all the confusion stirred up by four tickets, the Democrats were still able to recapture the House in 1860 which they had lost in 1858. Their hold on the Senate was not even threatened. The Supreme Court was safely Democratic. There may be probability, although there can be no certainty, that Lincoln would have been elected in a three-cornered contest. But had he been victorious, with the legislative and the judicial arms against him, could he have done more than the Whig Presidents of a decade and more ago? This is all in the realm of conjecture. But John Brown was dead and the likelihood of other forays exists only in the imagination. Had the nation held together and experienced the ineptitudes of what would have been Lincoln's helpless minority administration, the fears might have been quieted; and the South, with its control of the Congress might have continued to exercise its accustomed rule.

But no, the Democrats destroyed the instrument of accommodation they had used effectively for thirty years rather than exhaust its possibilities, and in so doing they precipitated the catastrophe which was to follow. Their invention was smashed because a large faction, mainly from the South, found it no longer useful. The party must try something else to serve their purposes.

The Douglas wing had nothing else to use so they clung desperately to it. The Southern wing had the ghost of Calhoun and set forth to make use of it. They would keep power in the states by seceding from Charleston and Baltimore. If they were defied by the North they would create a new power—just how they would use it, its engineers hardly knew—but the purpose generally was to insure for themselves, somehow, a position of power, autonomy, and security within a reorganized Union. Unfortunately Calhoun

was not alive to lead them; and the steps they took were haphaz-
ard, badly planned, and undertaken under circumstances that almost insured failure. Had they been able to enlist their entire
strength—fifteen states plus the city of Washington—and had
they been able to resist the temptation to assault Sumter, there is
a chance they might have won. But Calhoun was dead, and Lincoln
very much alive. They had not realized their potential—only
seven of the fifteen slave states had seceded. The ratio of manpower
and resources was very much against them. They had no navy.
They must bear the onus of slavery, and they had fired on the flag.
The odds, physical and psychological, were just too heavy. From
John Brown's raid to Sumter the course of Southern leadership
included an unhappy series of unfortunate decisions. In the name
of seeking security and their rights they had temporarily destroyed
their own creation. Neither they nor anybody else after this long
convention experience of shrinking leadership could have foreseen
that the prairie galoot from distant Illinois could in any sense prove
to be a messiah.

Had the nation followed its original intent and had no President,
the republic would have been governed by the legislative arm in
which factions of lawmakers, representing state organizations
rather than any nationally organized parties, would have operated.
Had these factions been unable to agree and had they developed
severe group hostility, if their constituencies had withdrawn from
the confederation, there might have been no resistance to this
secession as there was no executive to make decisions. However
this eventuality might well have destroyed the great republic and
put in its place a Balkanized society or something like present-day
Africa.

As the turbulent year of 1859 had drawn to its close the New
York socialite diarist George Templeton Strong recorded in his
voluminous daily commentary: "It's a sick nation, and I fear it
must be worse before it's better. The growing, vigorous North
must sooner or later assert its right to equality with the stagnant,
semi-barbarous South, and that assertion must bring on a struggle
and convulsion. It must come. Pity it could not be postponed some
twenty years, when Northern preponderance would be over-

whelming. If Northern abolitionism precipitate the crisis and force the battle on us *now,* it will be a fearful and doubtful contest." [1]

Had a Southern diarist been commenting at this time he might have written a paraphrase of the above. "This republic has been corrupted and it must be purged of its corruption. The civilized South, cultured in its rural felicity, must maintain its equality with the growing, rapacious North, and that exertion must bring on a struggle and convulsion. It must come. It must come soon before Northern preponderance becomes overwhelming. Northern abolitionism may precipitate the crisis and force the battle on us now; it will be a fearful and doubtful contest."

The Democrats at Charleston and Baltimore had realized that changing conditions were in fact pointing to the emergence of a new establishment governed by a new power based on a new consensus. Despite the demonstration of experience from 1776 to 1860 that Americans possessed the capacity to rule and shape the United States, through the instrumentation of Congress and partisan conventions, in 1860 that capacity failed. It failed because its operators lost faith in its efficiency. Instead of using the convention as an instrument of adjustment and the creation of consensus, they destroyed it. They destroyed it because they did not trust it any longer. They had lost their faith because of fear, conscience, a sense of honor, bad health, and a complicated series of personal antagonisms built up over years of association in Congress, conventions, and the peculiar environment of Washington. The Democratic party broke up because of a complex series of personal failures where, in an intricate system of group dynamics, people entrusted with responsibility for leadership could not measure up to the demands of the perilous times. The most spectacular evidence of this failure was the destruction of the Democratic party by its own managers. Calhoun had always disliked and distrusted the device employed to destroy him. It was his following who thirty years later scrapped it.

1 Allan Nevins and Milton Halsey Thomas (eds.), *The Diary of George Templeton Strong* (4 vols.; New York, 1952), II, 480.

Comment on

WHY THE DEMOCRATIC PARTY DIVIDED

Robert W. Johannsen

In his discussion of the question, "Why did the Democratic party divide?" Dean Nichols has emphasized the development and ultimate breakdown of party machinery and has sought to explain the demise of the Democracy in terms of individual and group behavior and human failure. This is a subject on which he can speak with the confidence and assurance of an authority. Dean Nichols' books spanning the 1850's, from his discussion of the operation of the Democratic machine early in the decade, through the administration of Franklin Pierce, to the disruption of American democracy, are widely recognized as classics of American history. Indeed, in the last volume of the trilogy he essayed to answer, in powerful detail, the very question under consideration this morning.

The destruction of the Democratic party in the spring of 1860, he has told us, was the result of human failure, of a disastrous failure of leadership. The party convention, the "instrument of accommodation" which Democrats had utilized for three decades in the interest of party unity, was abandoned and destroyed. The culprits producing this result, we are told, were the Southern delegates, comprising the professional leadership of the South, who shattered the party because it could no longer serve their purposes. They were men who did not measure up to the demands of their times.

The failure of the Charleston convention and the resultant

destruction of the Democratic party *was* to a large degree a tragedy of miscalculations. The politicians who thought they had full control of the situation had, in fact, lost control of it. The grim solidarity of Southern delegates against Douglas and his platform had not been anticipated in the camp of the Illinois Senator. The Douglas men felt that a "little eruption" in the convention was inevitable, but they were naïvely confident that any walkout would involve only a few delegates, possibly only the Alabama delegation. Such a small withdrawal would, they thought, redound to their advantage, for it would rid the convention of the hotheads and obstructionists who stood in the way of Douglas' nomination. The actual withdrawal of delegates from eight Southern states staggered the Douglas managers. Following the withdrawal, delegates from New York and some of the border states secured the approval of their interpretation of the two-thirds rule, thereby frustrating any possibility that Douglas could be nominated by those who remained. These delegates, misjudging the determination of the Little Giant's supporters, hoped to provide a "bridge" between the Douglas men and the bolters and thus reunite the party. The seceders, on their part, were persuaded that their action would force new concessions from the convention, that Douglas would be forced to withdraw his candidacy in favor of a man and a platform that was more acceptable to the South. But the olive branch was never extended. Instead, the Southerners received the unexpected news that the convention, unable to make a nomination, had adjourned to meet in Baltimore six weeks hence. When the delegates left Charleston, the party of Andrew Jackson had been reduced to a shambles.

But while the failure of the Charleston convention was due in part to miscalculation and to a failure of leadership, it was also the result of the calculated policy of a group of Southern politicians. Men like Charleston's fire-eating newspaper editor Robert Barnwell Rhett had months before laid plans for the breakup of the convention; one week before the delegates gathered, he had written the party's obituary, declaring that the Democratic party "is dead," without a "single principle common to its members North and South."

Chicago as the choice for the Republican convention of 1860 was,

I believe, referred to as "neutral ground." Charleston, South Carolina, was anything but neutral ground for the Democratic party; and any attempt to explain the division of the Democratic party must take this into account. The Douglasites were painfully aware that what they called the "outside pressure" would be against them at Charleston. Some effort was made to persuade the national committee to shift the site at the last moment. Both Baltimore and New Orleans were mentioned as locations more congenial to Douglas' candidacy. Failing this, the Douglas managers sought to induce as many Douglas men as possible to travel to Charleston —some states appointed twice as many delegates as they had votes, each delegate to cast half a vote; others appointed large numbers of alternate delegates. But the combination of Charleston's high lodging prices and the unusual length of the convention defeated this effort. The convention lasted ten days and long before its adjournment many Northern delegates had run out of money and returned home. During the last few days, the most crucial of the convention, the Charlestonians had the field to themselves— demonstrating wildly and noisily on behalf of those who engineered the walkout. Many wavering Southern delegates joined the bolters because of the strength of this outside pressure.

Granted, however, that this last conclave of a united Democratic party was destroyed in part because of human failure and misjudgement, one must still ask these questions: What was the context of this failure? What were the issues that forced this failure? Were there forces at work which *no* leadership, however adept, could by 1860 control? Although Dean Nichols alludes to these questions, I should like to explore a little more some elements that contribute to their answers.

When the Southern delegates walked out of the Charleston convention, they did so in protest against the adoption of the Douglas, or popular sovereignty, platform. Some did so out of an extreme and bitter dislike for the Illinois Senator; others acted because they could not accept a platform they deemed to be hostile to the interests of the South. In any case, Stephen A. Douglas and popular sovereignty, two forces that had by 1860 become indistinguishable, must loom large in any attempt to explain the fatal division in the Democratic party. Although the platform was the pretext of the walkout, it could not be separated from the person with whose name it had been so closely identified during the preceding decade. Douglas, one observer commented, was the "pivot individual" of the meeting.

Popular sovereignty, Douglas' formula for settling the increasingly troublesome territorial question, had never been fully accepted by the South. To Douglas, popular sovereignty meant that the territories, as territories, could determine the status of slavery within their bounds for themselves. The South never conceded this interpretation, insisting instead that such a decision over slavery could be made only when the territories moved into statehood. This fundamental disagreement was successfully obscured during the 1850's, partly because the South never advanced its position in a clear and unequivocal manner. To be sure, Southern leaders gave frequent lip service to Calhoun's insistence on equal rights for the South in the territories; but it was not until early in 1860, when the showdown appeared imminent, that a strong, explicit Southern platform was presented to the nation. At that time, Mississippi's Senator Jefferson Davis introduced his slave code resolutions, calling for the positive federal protection of slavery in the territories. The slave code proposal was not new to the South or to the party. Twelve years before, in 1848, the Democratic convention was convulsed by the same disagreement that shattered the party in 1860. Then it was the "squatter sovereignty" of Lewis Cass's Nicholson Letter and William L. Yancey's slave protectionist "Alabama Platform" that threatened to tear the party apart. The party convention, however, rejected the extreme Southern position; and party unity, more apparent than real, was preserved. Eight years later, at its Cincinnati convention, the party adopted a platform that glossed over the differences in interpretation between Douglas and the South, a tactic made necessary by the furor over the Kansas-Nebraska Act. Southern leaders acquiesced in a vaguely worded declaration that would enable each group to argue its own position without fear of contradicting the party statement. It was, as the South came to realize in 1860, little more than a "subterfuge."

Developments between 1856 and 1860 rendered the continued acquiescence of Southern leaders in such a policy highly unlikely.

The South was placed more clearly on the defensive in its struggle to maintain its position within the Union. Kansas was lost to slavery following the prolonged and bitter debate over the Lecompton constitution. The victory achieved in the Dred Scott decision had been dimmed by furious Republican opposition and by Douglas' "Freeport doctrine." The increasing strength of Northern Republicans was made more ominous by the realization that the census of 1860 would further emphasize the South's status as a minority section. John Brown's raid, occurring on the eve of the election year, seemed to demonstrate the jeopardy in which Southern institutions had been placed. A new and unmistakable Southern declaration was called for. Popular sovereignty, in any form, could no longer serve the interests of the South, if indeed it ever had. To one South Carolinian, popular sovereignty had become more dangerous to the South than Seward's "irrepressible conflict," for Douglas' doctrine was nothing more than abolition "in an offensive disguise." Southern leaders were determined to achieve a "pure" statement of Southern policies and desires, one that could not be variously interpreted, one over which there could be no question of meaning or definition. There must be, they said, no "dodges —no double constructions." The slave code resolutions, presented to the United States Senate in February, 1860, were both advice and warning to the Charleston convention. The South gave notice of its determination to have its way; either the party must reflect the Southern platform or the party must be abandoned. The territorial question, that disruptive legacy of manifest destiny, had become abstract and emotionalized, but it was to the South a question of vital significance. To more and more Southerners, the territories constituted the first line of defense for Southern civilization itself.

There was little doubt in the minds of Southern leaders in 1860 who their enemy was. Although Douglas' candidacy had been supported by the South in the Cincinnati convention, the Illinois Senator had become totally unacceptable to that section by 1860. His role in the conflict of the Buchanan administration had made his name anathema to the South. Douglas' unforgivable defiance of the administration and of the South and his unabashed alliance with Congressional Republicans in the Lecompton crisis had demonstrated his untrustworthiness as a spokesman for Southern interests. His crime was compounded in 1858 when, at Freeport, Illinois, he advised the territories on how they might circumvent the Dred Scott decision. No matter how the Supreme Court had ruled or might rule, the territories could still effectively bar slavery from their borders. The next year, he destroyed whatever strength he might yet have had in the South when he published his important essay on popular sovereignty in *Harper's Magazine*. The South was quick to act. In the Senate, Douglas was stripped of his longtime chairmanship of the territorial committee, and to one Alabama Congressman, he was now "outside the pale of the party." Douglas not only faced the undisguised hostility of the South but he also confronted the strong personal antagonism of the Buchanan administration. At Charleston, both groups combined to defeat Douglas at any price. So strong was the animus against Douglas that Alexander H. Stephens placed the breakup of the Democratic party solely on this personal basis. The Southern bolters, he wrote in September, 1860, "ran not from a platform but from a man. . . . The whole rupture originated in personal ambition, spite and hate."

But there was more involved in the Charleston disaster than a vital difference on the territorial question or personal hatred. The "fatal impasse," as Dean Nichols has called it, was also the result of a struggle for party leadership. The seeds of Democratic disruption had actually been sown many years before, at least as far back as 1844 when Martin Van Buren, the heir of Jacksonian Democracy, was passed over by the party's convention in favor of James K. Polk. From that time on, the Democratic party became increasingly oriented toward the South. The withdrawal of the Van Buren forces from the party in 1848 and the movement of Southern Whigs into the party in later years enhanced its growing Southern character. The emergence of the Republican party from the confusion that followed the Kansas-Nebraska Act further weakened the Democratic party in the North. At the same time, the fact that Northern Democrats were forced to compete for votes with Republicans (who had no Southern brethren to worry about) necessitated the adoption of a more national, less Southern party outlook. In 1848, popular sovereignty had been endorsed as a "national" solution to the territorial question. Douglas, the recognized leader of the Northwestern Democracy, sought in the 1850's to establish the Democratic party firmly on the foundation of popular sovereignty. This doctrine, he thought, should be one on which both North and South could unite; its adoption as a Democratic party line would enable Northern Democrats to combat the "sectional" appeal of the Republican party and would halt the "sectional" trend in the Democratic party itself. Indeed, popular sovereignty seemed to Douglas the only basis on which the Democratic party could maintain its national supremacy.

During the last four years of the decade, Douglas' effort was converted into a Northwestern revolt against Southern leadership in the party. Political survival for Douglas and his followers depended upon the degree to which they could disassociate themselves from the Southern extreme. Douglas' stand on the Lecompton constitution, his "Freeport doctrine," his *Harper's* essay were all attempts to strengthen the Democracy in the North, to offer what he thought was a national position on the question of the day, and to halt the sectionalization of political parties that he knew could only be fatal to the nation itself. To Douglas, the struggle at Charleston was a struggle for political survival for himself as well as his party. Acquiescence in a Southern platform would be political suicide for Northern Democrats. Already smarting from Republican charges that they were minions of the slavocracy, they were placed in an impossible position by the demands and actions of the party's Southern leaders. "We are not in a condition to carry another ounce of Southern weight," wrote one of Douglas' close associates.

In the interest of maintaining party unity, Douglas offered the formula that had succeeded four years before. He would, he said, accept the Cincinnati platform again, "ready to reaffirm it at Charleston without the change of a word" and giving it "the same construction we have always given it." Later he suggested that an endorsement of the Dred Scott decision be added to it. But the South knew only too well that Douglas' "construction" of the Cincinnati platform was not their "construction" and that the Dred Scott decision was also interpreted differently by the Illinois Senator. They would not, they insisted, accept another subterfuge.

They would gain little by such a strategy. Nor could Douglas and the Northwestern Democrats accede to the Southern demand for a slave code. "I firmly believe I am right," Douglas wrote to a Georgian, "and cannot change my opinions at this late day even to be President." The issue had to be met in an unequivocal fashion; neither side would budge and a showdown was inevitable. Here, then, was the irrepressible conflict—within the Democratic party itself.

What was the impact of the Democratic split on subsequent events? The breakup of the party at Charleston did more than simply guarantee the election of a sectional President. The destruction of the Democracy sealed the fate of the Union itself. It removed from national politics the last remaining national party; party politics had become sectionalized. The safety of the Union depended upon the ability of the Democratic party to adjust its differences; as the effort failed there was little hope for the nation.

Douglas, of course, did not give up. Following his nomination at Baltimore in June, he embarked on a strenuous and unprecedented campaign tour, stumping the sections where he had least chance for success. His appeal was not so much for votes for President but was rather an attempt to persuade Democrats in New England and the border states that he and not the Southerner Breckinridge was the true leader of the party. The campaign of 1860 was a campaign to reorganize the Democratic party under strong Northwestern, and hence, in Douglas' mind, national leadership. He peremptorily rejected all suggestions that the Douglas and Breckinridge presidential tickets fuse in some Northern states. "Any Compromise with the Secessionists," he wrote, "would be ruinous." Lincoln's election was only a temporary setback to his plans. "Four years will soon pass away," he told an audience. In the meantime, he saw as his duty the restoration of the Democratic party as a sound, national organization. The failure of the Union during the crisis months of the secession winter delivered a fatal blow to Douglas' vision. The destruction of the Democratic party at Charleston had been an event of greater significance than even Douglas had realized.

The party machinery, the development of which Dean Nichols has traced so well, proved inadequate to the difficult task of maintaining party unity in 1860. Was this failure solely because of a failure in leadership? Undoubtedly this was a large factor; but something must also be said for the divisive forces that had been building up over the years, for the issues and antagonisms that had become deeply rooted in men's minds, of the yawning gorge that separated North and South, of the misunderstanding, distortion, and emotionalism that had attached to the dividing sections. The nation survived the Democratic party by only a few months, giving credence to Douglas' contention that a strong, united Democracy was the only sure guarantee of national union. Both party and nation suffered the same fate—strained to the breaking point, incapable of resolving their issues within a normal framework of operation. Fatal weaknesses in both were exposed and laid bare. As men preferred to destroy their party, their "instrument of accommodation," rather than confront the alternatives of compromise or surrender, so also did the American people on the larger scene seem to believe that the issues they faced could only be settled outside the normal workings of democratic government. Party failed and nation failed—by 1860, both had passed the point of no return.

III

WHY THE SOUTHERN STATES SECEDED

Avery O. Craven

On December 14, 1860, a conservative Georgia editor stated in terms, which he evidently supposed everyone would understand and accept, the reasons why the Southern states were seceding from the Union. "It is a mistake," he said, "to suppose that it is the mere election of Lincoln, without regard to anything else, that has driven the States of the South into their present resistance, and their present determination to seek that safety and security out of the Union which they have been unable to obtain within it."

What that "anything else" was, he then made clear. "The election of Lincoln," he said, "is merely the confirmation of a purpose which the South had hoped would be abanboned by the opponents of slavery in the North. It is a declaration that they mean to carry out their aggressive and destructive policy, weakening the institution at every point where it can be assailed either by legislation or by violence, until, in the brutal language of Charles Sumner, 'it dies like a poisoned rat in its hole.' "

The things to be noticed in this bald statement are, that Northern aggression consisted primarily in the determination to put the institution of Negro slavery on the road to ultimate extinction; that Lincoln's election made the carrying out of that policy both possible and probable; and that the Southern states, much against their wills, had been forced to seek "that safety and security" for their peculiar institution, outside the Union, which they had a perfectly good constitutional right to expect within it.

Most Southerners agreed that Republican hostility to slavery and the evidence of wide Northern approval in Lincoln's election justified secession. They somehow felt that the real question before the people in the recent election had not been whether Breckinridge or Lincoln, Bell or Douglas should be President, but whether slavery be perpetuated or abolished. As one writer said: "No man of common sense, who is not prepared to surrender the institution of slavery with the safety and independence of the South can doubt that the time for action has come—now or never!" Some saw the economic danger ahead. "It was not safe," they said, "to trust eight hundred million dollars worth of negroes in the hands of a power that says we do not own the property, that the title under the Constitution is bad, and under the law of God still worse." "Slave property," they agreed, "is the foundation of all property in the South. When security in this is shaken, all other property partakes of its instability."

Others objected to the Republican boast of moral superiority. They placed "honor" above "interest." They resented less what the Republicans had done or might do, than the things they said and the self-righteous way in which they said them. They could shrug off the material threats, but they could no longer endure the "untiring efforts" to degrade the South in the eyes of all who came within their reach—denying the piety of their clergy and calling their Congressmen "desperadoes" less worthy of trust than "the inmates of our penitentiaries." The question of honor was "paramount to all others."

But more than abstract honor was involved. Republican victory in 1860 was not just a temporary slip. The South had fallen steadily behind the North in population and, denied expansion, was losing political equality as well. The Republican threat to a way of life was bad enough. To lose all hope of an equal voice in national affairs was even worse. As one desperate Southerner said: "Rather than to surrender Southern equality in the Union, let our slaves be lost . . . our fields be desolated . . . our blood to flow" but "never, never should her people . . . yield this most precious of all earthly possessions—their feeling of self-respect."

2

The official statements made by the seceding conventions in their appeal to the rest of mankind for a sympathetic understanding of their "momentous step" also stressed first of all the threat to their "domestic institutions." The election of a sectional President, "pledged to principles and a policy which we regard as repugnant to the Constitution . . . beget[s] a feeling of insecurity which . . . alarm[s] a people jealous of their rights." The Southern states were now a helpless minority "in imminent peril, being in the power of a majority, reckless of Constitutional obligations and pledged to principles leading to [their] destruction."

Some complained of the exclusion of their citizens from territories "owned in common by all the States" and of Northern approval of John Brown's raid, but the one grievance above all others was the refusal to return fugitive slaves. This refusal proved beyond all doubt that neither the Constitution of the United States, nor the Acts of Congress, nor the decisions of the Supreme Court could longer be relied upon as protection for Southern rights.

The final, and perhaps the most powerful emotional factor in the situation, was brought out by a speaker in the Alabama convention.

Mr. President [he began] if pecuniary loss alone were involved in the abolition of slavery, I should hesitate long to give the vote I now intend to give. If the destruction of slavery entailed on us poverty alone, I could bear it, for I have seen poverty and felt its sting. But poverty, Mr. President, would be one of the least of evils that would befall us from the abolition of African slavery. There are now in the slaveholding states over four million slaves; dissolve the relation of master and slave, and what, I ask, would become of that race? To remove them from among us is impossible. History gives us no account of the exodus of such a number of persons. We neither have a place to which to remove them, nor the means of such removal. They, therefore, must remain with us; and if the relation of master and slave be dissolved, and our slaves be turned loose amongst us without restraint, they would either be destroyed by our own hands—the hands to which they look, and look with confidence for protection—or we ourselves would become demoralized and degraded.

Nor was there any reason to hope that the war on slavery would ever cease. As one editor put it: "The settled hostility of the Northern people must become stronger with each year. The present dominant party in the Free States, based upon the single idea of opposition to the extension, spread, or existence of slavery, now numbering in its ranks nearly two million voters, will become more powerful as the sentiment upon which it is founded gains strength and intensity. It has now secured the President. In two years more, at most, it will have both Houses of Congress. Then the Supreme Court will be reorganized . . . and we shall have 'no more Dred Scott decisions.' "

As the Reverend Benjamin M. Palmer told his people: "A whole generation has been educated to look upon the system of slavery with abhorrence as a national blot. They hope, and look, and pray for its extinction within a reasonable time, and cannot be satisfied unless things are seen drawing to that conclusion." It had thus become perfectly clear that the North either "could not let slavery alone," or "would not," or did not "intend to let it alone." It was just as clear, they said, that the "Black Republican victory of November [was] incontrovertible proof of a diseased and dangerous public opinion all over the North, and a certain forerunner of further and more atrocious aggression."

3

There had been serious crises in national affairs at other times and Southerners had, more than once, threatened secession. But never before had there been such an atmosphere of desperation and finality, such intense realization of impending disaster, such a feeling of helplessness in the face of what seemed to be a driving force against which resistance had all along been hopeless. Lincoln's election did not present an immediate threat, but it did indicate that a new and final stage in the slavery struggle had been reached. Seemingly the nation had got itself into such a predicament that no one, however well meaning, could check the drift towards the use of force.

Up until the John Brown raid, there had been much Southern protest and indignation because of Northern criticism of slavery and because of denial of equality in the territories and in the distribution of governmental favors. But there had been little panic and much confidence in the Southern politician's ability to protect his section, confidence in Northern friends, and in the Democratic party. Now all was changed. Talk of the "irrepressible conflict" and of "the higher law" now meant something. The Republican party, a strange mixture of moral values and sectional economic interests, had triumphed in a national election. Stephen A. Douglas had been forced to interpret his squatter sovereignty doctrine in accordance with the views of his Northern supporters, and the South's desperate gamble at Charleston to control the Democratic party, to secure federal protection of slavery in the territories, and to force the Northern Democracy back under Southern control, had failed. The game had been lost and submission or secession were the only choices left.

For the first time the Southerner had to face the serious realities of life in a slaveholding society. He had to recognize the possibility of ultimate emancipation. He had to calculate the financial risk of having millions of dollars invested in slaves swept away; face the frightening possibility of bloody racial readjustment; be content with permanent political impotence if three-fifths of his slaves were no longer counted as population; and, above all, accept the harsh, cold fact that he stood alone in a world which insisted that slavery was both an economic burden and a moral outrage.

Other issues now lost their importance. Every decision had to be made according to the demands of slavery, and slavery alone. The only defense against economic, social, and political ruin lay in placing slavery beyond the reach of its enemies. The South had been driven into a corner. The choice between submission and secession would have to be made sooner or later.

Abraham Lincoln had understood the Southern dilemma and had talked of removing the economic difficulty by compensated emancipation and the social-racial problem by removing the Negro from the country. He had once framed a bill for these purposes. But nothing had come from his thinking; and the Republican threat, in Southern eyes, was the old abolition threat to deal with slavery as a sin to be removed by the usual revival technique of conviction, repentance, and voluntary and immediate renunciation. The resulting problems were not to be taken into consideration.

The idea that some concessions or some plan such as Lincoln had suggested might have saved the day at this late date overlooks two important considerations. At no time after the early 1830's is there a single shred of evidence to show that any number of planters, intoxicated by the notion that "Cotton was King," would have surrendered a single slave for any consideration ever suggested. It was now too late even if it had once been possible— which is doubtful. Nor would the abolitionist at any time have considered such a proposal. As one editor put it: "The disease is too deep seated. The election of Mr. Lincoln to the Presidency, gives a tremendous onward impulse to anti-slavery sentiment. He rides a wave he cannot control or guide to conservative results, even if so disposed."

4

The historian attempting to answer the question as to why the Southern states seceded must recognize the predicament into which the nation had fallen. He must understand that the Southern states were right when they said that their domestic institutions were no longer safe in the Union. They erred only in not recognizing the more important fact that their institutions were not safe anywhere in the nineteenth century and the emerging modern world. They were blind, also, in not realizing that secession was no remedy for their troubles in this age of growing national consolidation. They would find out, after four bloody years of heroic fighting, that organization, efficiency, technology, and urban industrialism win wars in this age regardless of individual courage and sacrifice.

The historian must also understand that Lincoln, in turn, was toying with the impossible when he said that slavery, where it existed, would be safe under his administration. He could not have checked the agitation against slavery; nor could he have guaranteed the return of fugitive slaves. These were the things the South was demanding. He should have known that in the United States an institution which he himself had said was morally wrong could not much longer be legally right. William H. Seward showed a far better understanding of the Republican party when he insisted that all human law "must be brought to the standard of the law of God . . . and must stand or fall by it." Charles Sumner saw the situation more clearly than either Lincoln or Seward when he said: "They have proclaimed slavery to be *wrong,* and have pledged themselves with force against its extension. It is difficult to sense how they can longer sustain themselves *merely* on that grounds. Their promise sustains a broader conclusion, that is, the duty of no longer allowing the *continuance* of evil anywhere within our Constitutional action. They must become Abolitionists."

The abolitionists themselves had understood this and resolved that the Republican position on "the folly and wrong of slavery," from which they drew "only the modest inference" that it ought not to be allowed to spread, really implied that "it ought not to be tolerated anywhere." It should also be recalled that both Seward and Lincoln had brought the moral issue into politics and used it to advance their political fortunes. Seward had talked of "the higher law" and "the irrepressible conflict," and Lincoln had insisted on the necessity of opposing Stephen A. Douglas, practical politician, because he, Douglas, had been foolish enough to say that he did not care whether the people of a territory voted slavery up or down, even though he knew and Lincoln knew that they would vote it down. In so doing, they had lifted the issue to the abstract level of right versus wrong and had thereby created a situation with which the democratic process of toleration and compromise could not deal. Only force would answer.

5

With this much accepted, the historian must then remember that the final centering on antislavery aggression as the sum total of Southern complaints was only the last stage in a long series of developments. Somewhere in the years after 1815, the South began taking over from the North the role of "the abused." In the emerging era when progress was beginning to be measured in terms of industry, cities, and complex finances, some Southern spokesmen saw the inevitable growth of federal power and the corresponding decline of the agricultural South. They foresaw the day when the South would be reduced to that colonial status described, in 1860, as one, in which "Yankees" monopolized "the carrying trade with its immense profits, all the importing, [and] most of the exporting business for the whole Union. . . . New York City, like a mighty queen of commerce, sits proudly upon her island throne, sparkling in jewels and waving an undisputed commercial scepter over the

South. By means of her railways and navigable streams, she sends out her long arms to the extreme South, and with avidity rarely equaled, grasps our gains and transfers them to herself—taxing us at every step—and depleting us as extensively as possible without actually destroying us."

And the reason for this, they charged, was that "the whole policy of the Federal Government, from the beginning [had] been to build up and enrich the North at Southern expense. In this business, the monster engine, a high Protective Tariff, [had] been the chief instrument." And besides this, there had been the "fishing bounties, and the navigation laws, and the giving away the public lands, millions of acres at a time, all of which tend[ed] to aggrandise the Northern section of the Union." Stated the Charleston *Mercury,* "On every living issue deemed vital to the South, the Northern members, as a body, [have been] against the South."

John Taylor of Caroline, in Virginia, had early talked this way; and Robert Turnbull, in South Carolina, had brought it to a climax in nullification days. Both denounced the tariff and the "consolidation" trends which permitted its passage. Both viewed it as a violation of the Constitution and as a conflict between economic interests. As Turnbull wrote in denouncing the tariff as "the recent exercise of powers never contemplated by the framers of the Constitution, . . . the more National and less Federal the Government becomes, the more certainly will the interests of the great majority of the states be promoted, but with the same certainty, will the interests of the South be depressed and destroyed." The interest of the North and West was "that the Government should become more and more National," while the interest of the South was "that it should continue Federal."

For this reason Northern statesmen were "not astute to enquire" as to whether an act was in keeping with "the clear intent and meaning of the Constitution." They did not tremble at such violations. Only the South had an interest in checking unconstitutional acts and in keeping the nation federal in character.

Thus for its interests and its safety, Turnbull insisted that the South must forever oppose the implied powers of Congress. The interests of the North and West would always lead them toward "usurpation" and departure from the social compact. They had no reason to quarrel with an expanding national government which was building *their* industry with unconstitutional tariffs, and *their* commerce with unconstitutional internal improvements. Bitterly Turnbull noted that "we hear of no projects in Congress to tax the manufactures of the North to support the agriculture of the South." It was all the other way around.

Alexis de Tocqueville, too, had seen such a situation as marking the end of our federal system. "States form confederations," he wrote, "in order to derive equal advantages from their union. . . . If one of the federated states acquire a preponderance sufficiently great to enable it to take exclusive possession of the central authority, it will . . . cause its own supremacy to be respected under the name of the sovereignty of the Union. Great things may then be done in the name of the Federal Government, but in reality that Government will have ceased to exist."

6

The tariff, however, in spite of its sectional character, poorly explained the growing inferiority and colonial status of the South as a section. Nor could Southern unity be secured in opposition. Too many Southerners were longing for a diversified economic life, and too many saw other reasons for the South's plight. "Why are we so far behind in the great march of improvement," asked one citizen. "Simply because we have failed to act in obedience to the dictates of sound policy. Simply because we have been almost criminally neglectful of our own interests." Another said, "You may nullify the tariff, but you cannot nullify the fertile soils of Alabama and Mississippi."

And so the tariff issue lost much of its appeal with the failure of nullification. South Carolina had stood alone. Her warning to the South had been in vain. In time the industrialists of the North and the planters of the South would join hands in shaping the nation's tariff schedules.

In the meantime, John C. Calhoun, unabashed and unenlightened by his nullification experience, had taken up where Turnbull left off. In the early 1830's he had come forward with the assertion that Negro slavery, as practiced in the South, was "a positive good." He followed this, in 1837, with what was ultimately to

become the fatal Southern orthodox platform. In a series of resolutions offered in the Senate, December 27, he insisted on the
strictly federal character of our government in which the states had
retained their sovereignty and "the exclusive and sole right over
their own domestic institutions and police"; that "any meddling
of any one or more States, or a combination of their citizens, with
the domestic institutions and police of the others, on any grounds,
or under any pretext whatever, political, moral or religious, with
a view to their alteration or subversion, is an assumption of superiority, not warranted by the Constitution:—insulting to the States
interfered with,—tending to endanger their domestic peace and
tranquility."

This government, he said, had been founded to give increased
stability and security to the domestic institutions of the states; and
since slavery was such a Southern institution, "no change of opinion
or feeling, on the part of other states . . . in relation to it, can
justify them or their citizens in open and systematic attacks thereon,
with a view to its overthrow." He closed with the assertion that
efforts to abolish slavery in the District of Columbia on the pretext
"that it is immoral or sinful" would be an attack on the institutions
of all slaveholding states; while the effort to check its expansion
into the territories would be a denial of Southern equality in the
Union.

Here was an implied ultimatum to the effect that the permanence
of the Union depended on the universal acceptance of the sovereignty of the states in a federal system and of the positive good of
Negro slavery above criticism. It was a demand which men who
had caught stride with the oncoming modern world, even though
not yet clearly conscious of its full meaning, could not possibly
accept. It would, however, cause them to pause and to think, and
instinctively to resist. Interests and morals were both involved.

Calhoun's extreme demands, and his blindness or indifference to
the nationalistic and democratic-humanitarian character of the age
in which he lived had exactly the opposite effects from those he
had intended. Already his shortsighted efforts to check antislavery
petitions had enabled John Quincy Adams to bring a sacred American right to the support of the hitherto rather ineffective abolition
movement. His next equally rash and shortsighted move to annex

Texas solely on grounds of safety to Southern institutions, linked slavery and expansion, pushed the issue into politics, and created the impression that there was a "slave power" bent on spreading its peculiar institution by every means possible to every corner of the nation. Its ultimate purpose was just "to lug new slave states in" and thereby gain political control. A new and wider antislavery appeal was thus available; its political possibilities were greatly expanded.

Calhoun and his supporters, it would seem, were bent on proving true all that the abolitionists had charged. By not understanding the fact that they were fighting an age, not just a group of fanatics, they had alarmed and aroused the whole North. Joshua Giddings in Congress was thereby enabled, with wide approval, to charge that the North was "politically bound, hand and foot, surrendered to the rule and government of a slave-holding oligarchy." He could insist, with equal support, that "our tariff is as much an anti-slavery measure as the rejection of Texas. So is the subject of internal improvements and the distribution of the proceeds of the public lands. The advocates of perpetual slavery oppose all of them, they regard them as opposed to the interests of slavery." Blundering Southern leadership had thus placed their section squarely across the path of what Northern men had begun to think of as progress. They were demanding that the world stand still.

7

When James K. Polk, Democrat and slaveholder, accepted war with Mexico but compromised the Oregon boundary, fostered a lower tariff and vetoed a river and harbor bill aimed primarily to aid the West, the North was ready with the Wilmot Proviso to check proslavery gains in the new territories. The sectional struggle shifted sharply from slavery *per se* to one of slavery expansion, and the bitter sectional crisis which quickly developed revealed the tragic condition into which the nation had fallen. A Southern movement, impossible before, spontaneously developed; and the call went out for a Southern convention. Talk of secession became common, and the charge of Northern disregard for the Constitution and her determination to monopolize the territories as a means of abolishing slavery was accepted without question. On the other side, Northern determination to check the spread of slavery and an awakened consciousness of slavery as a national disgrace were as marked and as positive.

The frantic efforts of patriots finally shifted the issues from abstractions to the concrete problems involved, and compromise became possible. But it did not come until Calhoun had again proclaimed the sovereignty of the states; had restated his charge of Northern aggression; and had made his demands for equal rights in the territories, the end of slavery agitation, the faithful observance of fugitive slave laws, and constitutional amendments to restore sectional equilibrium. He demonstrated again the fact that Southern leadership had remained largely untouched and unchanged by the facts and thoughts of the onrushing nineteenth century.

William H. Seward, by contrast, seized the opportunity to announce the arrival of that century. Bluntly he told his colleagues that they lived in a "consolidated Union" in which the states had "surrendered their equality as States, and submitted themselves to the sway of the numerical majority without qualifications or checks." He also informed them that the issues before them were moral issues: slavery was a sin and thus Americans could not "be either true Christians or real freemen if [they] impose[d] on another a chain [they] defi[ed] all human power to fasten on [themselves]." The demands for the return of fugitive slaves smacked of the Dark Ages, and our human laws must be brought "to the standards of the law of God. . . ."

Seward, in turn, was revealing the fact that the Northern mind and conscience had kept pace with the industry, the cities, the finance, and the railroads of the onrushing nineteenth century. He was making it equally clear that a realization of the dignity of a human being and a deep feeling of guilt for its violation were as marked as the material changes.

The Southern demand for a more efficient fugitive slave law which came out of the Compromise of 1850 again showed how poorly informed Southern leaders were and how inadequate was their understanding of the Northern mind. Nothing could have contributed more towards rendering slavery obnoxious. Nothing could have convinced the North so completely of Southern inhumanity and the calloused state of the Southern conscience as did this act. Yet strict Northern obedience was the condition on which the Southern states accepted the Compromise; and Northern refusal to comply with its enforcement constituted, in the end, almost the only concrete evidence offered in support of the charge of Northern aggression and of Northern lack of respect for the Constitution. As one said in 1860: "The only excuse for disunion, and the only reason that we deem the idea tolerable, is that the Constitution has been violated by the 'personal liberty acts' and negro-stealing mobs of the North, and that the election of a Black Republican will show that instead of fanaticism getting cool, it is growing worse, and, therefore the sooner the South gets clear from them the better."

"The Constitution," said another, "affords no remedy for Southern grievances. To the Southern people the Constitution is as worthless as a piece of waste paper so far as protection to the slavery interest is concerned. The Constitution authorizes slavery; the same instrument declares that fugitives shall be returned to their masters; Congress has passed laws in accordance therewith; and the decisions of the Supreme Court affirm and maintain the mandates of the Constitution and the laws of the National Legislature." Yet, as he said, if a master attempted to recover his servant in accord with his constitutional rights, he would be arrested, fined, and sent to prison in nine different Northern states. No wonder that the Reverend J. Thornwell insisted that the original Constitution had been repealed and new terms of Union submitted for Southern acceptance.

Yet, at this very moment, the Charleston *Mercury,* speaking for the only portion of the South eager for secession, was saying that the "Personal Liberty Laws" were not of the slightest consequence to the "Cotton States." "Few or none of our slaves are lost, by being carried away and protected from recapture in the Northern States." These laws only mattered "in the insult they conveyed to the South, and the evidence they offered of Northern faithlessness."

8

In the decade which followed the Compromise of 1850, the North as a whole moved rapidly forward into the modern world. It was a period "when modern industrial capitalism was beginning to sink its roots deep into the American economy." Northern cities both on the seaboard and far back in the interior were reaching metropolitan proportions. Canals and railroads were linking the Northeast and the Northwest closer together, and the coastal cities from Boston to Baltimore were competing for the Western produce which once went largely to New Orleans. The "young industrial capitalism of textiles, iron, machinery, wood, and leather products" was no longer content to be held back by the restrictions on protection, banking, labor supply, and public works imposed by the Democratic party under Southern influence. The hard, cold facts of economic and social interdependence were teaching them the value of national consolidation. The Union was an economic necessity.

Nor were they willing to see slavery spread to the territories of the farther West. Rather, the territories should be homesteaded by free men and women and made more accessible by government aid to rivers and harbors and railroads. It took only the fictitious Uncle Tom and the unfortunate Kansas-Nebraska Bill to bring into being the sectional Republican party as the carrier of their interests and their values. They did not clearly understand what they were doing, but they were, in fact, creating a political party which stood for the nationalism, the industrial capitalism, and the democratic-humanitarian impulses of the modern world.

9

The Southern states, meanwhile, followed their accustomed course. There were changes here as well as in the North, but they tended to strengthen old patterns, not to add new ones. More and more the cotton kingdom along the Gulf dominated the section. In spite of rather remarkable advances in the agriculture, industry, and transportation of the older states, "Cotton" increasingly spoke for the South. Its voice was more confident and more aggressive. Its planters had greater reasons for maintaining the status quo and more reason for fearing the attacks on slavery. The supreme confidence of its leaders in the power of cotton to make or break the prosperity of the whole Western world provided most of the confidence with which the whole South ultimately accepted the risks in secession. It was the cotton states' extreme demand for new guarantees for the protection of slavery in the territories which destroyed the Democratic party at Charleston.

Conservatives resented what they called "the fierce and eager instigations of the Cotton States"; and border state spokesmen insisted that the cotton states should "bear with the few wrongs inflicted upon them, until those, who 'lose ten times as many negroes and suffer ten times as many inconveniences through the hostility of the Northern people to their institutions,'" and "who stand between them and danger," should "feel it their duty and interest to act." Yet, in the end, those who had suffered most and would continue to suffer most, permitted those who had prospered most and suffered least to shape the section's destiny.

It was a University of Virginia professor who wrote at the time when secession was a reality:

Indignation and alarm alternate in my breast when I think of wretched little South Carolina, like an insolent and enfeebled reactionary, plunging the whole country into strife and confusion of which others must bear the brunt. . . . And when I reflect that the mean desertion of the other Southern States compels us to make this the crisis of our destiny, whether we like it or not, I am oppressed at once with indignation and anxiety. And these feelings are aggravated by the consideration that while I think the conspirators of the cotton states deserve the condign punishment, our safety makes it necessary that we should interpose to screen them if need be. . . . They bluster and threaten, safe, as they imagine, behind the intervening tiers of quiet Commonwealths to whose chivalrous feelings and sympathy they design to appeal to support them in a course abhorrent to the principles of these States and destructive to their interests.

Yet when Lincoln called for troops, the good professor was convinced that "nothing remains now to the Christian patriot but to strike strongly for the right, humbly invoking the aid and blessing of our fathers' God."

Thus under cotton's rule and with able assistance from the Northern abolitionists, from Seward, Sumner and John Brown, the few who from the beginning had wished to break up the Union found the opportunity to shift the Southern efforts from defense to aggression. They realized that it was not possible to dissolve the Union with "unanimity and without division." Said Barnwell Rhett, "Men having both nerve and self-sacrificing patriotism must head the movement and shape its course, controlling and compelling their inferior contemporaries." Deliberately they turned their backs on the nineteenth century. Closing their eyes to the tattered realities about them and their minds to all the democratic-humanitarian demands of the age in which they lived, they proclaimed the perfection of their ways and values and their superiority over those of all the Western world.

It was the North, they said, which was deluded. What its leaders called progress was, in fact, the real backwardness. Its boasted cities were breeders of crime and vice and social conflict. Its free labor system was nothing other than cruel, impersonal exploitation devoid of all responsibility. Its chaotic social-economic system was marked by periodic depressions, endless strife between capital and labor, and a constant threat of revolution. Its lack of stability had destroyed all respect for constitutional restrictions and had, at last, produced a sectional political party bent on national domination. It had produced an eroded people who would not fight even for their own interests.

In sharp contrast to all this, they pictured the South as a wholesome rural world, orthodox in religion and untroubled by the restless isms that beset the North. A peaceful world where capital and labor were one and where the realities of inequality between individuals and races were accepted and adjusted to the benefit of all. The institution of slavery, instead of being a blight upon the region, was the very foundation on which a superior civilization rested. Instead of debasing the character of the master, as charged, it produced the highest type of leader and a man who accepted his responsibilities both to his slaves and to society. Only in a slave society, where all white men were equal, was a true democracy possible. Only where the Negro was enslaved was he happy, productive, and free from the worry and cares of a complex civilization for which he was ill-fitted by nature. On the mudsills of slavery a golden age was alone possible, and all the world would one day accept the fact. The state, not the nation, should command first allegiance. The nineteenth century was moving in the wrong direction.

It is, indeed, difficult to believe that under normal conditions any considerable number of Southerners would have accepted the absurd notion either of Northern decadence or of Southern perfection. But nothing, in the 1850's, could long remain normal. In the North, change crowded on the heels of change; and public reaction to events, whether economic or political, no longer took form from the events themselves, but from the sectional slavery controversy. There might have been some question as to the actual danger of slavery expansion from the Kansas-Nebraska Act or the Dred Scott decision, but that did not matter. The issue was one of right or wrong. What did matter was that "the Slave Power" had been given the legal right to expand and that right brought a firm Northern determination to see slavery confined to its present limits and set on the road to ultimate extinction. The day for compromise with slavery had ended.

This grim Northern determination—when combined with the brutal fact that the South, in spite of its control of the Democratic party, had become a permanent political minority, its social system under moral condemnation by the whole Western world, its economic life, though prosperous, reduced to colonial dependence on Northern merchants and bankers—gave the Southern extremists a new lease on life. Critics stood almost helpless before the apprehensions, the fears, the indignation, and the self-respect to which the fanatics could appeal. "All that could be done by moderate, dispassionate, patriotic, and experienced men was to go with the current, endeavoring to subdue its boiling and seething energies. . . ."

By 1860, the extreme, self-appointed spokesmen for Southern rights had all but silenced their critics and sealed the Southern mind against all outside opinion. They were able to split the Democratic party with demands based on their assumptions of the rightness and perfection of the slavery system. With a curious psychopathic twist at the moment of decision in the Charleston convention, William L. Yancey of Alabama indignantly upbraided his Northern colleagues for treating slavery as an evil. They should have boldly pronounced it a positive good. If they had taken the position that slavery was right by the laws of nature and of God, they would have triumphed.

To this archaic demand, George E. Pugh of Ohio gave the only answer a modern man could give and the one that would be given over and over again: "Gentlemen of the South, you mistake us— you mistake us! We will not do it."

10

As the campaign of 1860 developed, a once conservative Southern editor impatiently brushed aside all projects for saving the Union. They were all "feeble and fruitless" because of the "absolute impossibility of revolutionizing Northern opinion in relation to slavery."

Without a change of heart, radical and thorough, all guarantees which might be offered are not worth the paper on which they would be enscribed. As long as slavery is looked upon by the North with abhorrence; as long as the South is regarded as a mere slave-breeding and slave-driving community; as long as false and pernicious theories are cherished respecting the inherent equality and rights of every human being, there can be no satisfactory political union between the two sections.

Northern editors were just as realistic. "We cannot tell Mr. Yancey," said one, "that we do not believe slavery wrong, for the reverse is the profound conviction of three-fourths of the whole North. . . . It would be dishonest to say that this conviction will not remain and grow stronger every day." And to promise the "complete revolution in the moral and political convictions" which the South demanded, or to promise that all opposition to slavery would cease, was like promising that "water shall run up hill and two and two shall make five." Another continued, "The strife between freedom and slavery . . . is but a fragment of the great conflict of [the] ages, the ever raging war between those things which are just, virtuous, useful, and good, and those which are hurtful and vicious and wrong."

Had not the struggle between the sections at bottom rested on such foundations as these, there might have been some way out. But as things stood, the mere election of Lincoln was "only confirmation of a purpose which the South had hoped would be abandoned by the opponents of Slavery in the North," and, which failing, drove the states of the South into "their present resistance, and their present determination to seek that safety and security out of the Union which they have been unable to obtain within it."

"In no other way," said a contemporary, "can we account for the perfect whirlwind of public feeling which swept everything before it, either utterly annihilating conservatism and nationality, or reducing to impotence the few who still ventured to make a timid appeal on behalf of the Union. . . ."

11

But this, after all, answers our question only in terms of the day. It ignores the fact that while there is strife and hatred "men have eyes for nothing save the fact that the enemy is the cause of all the troubles; but long, long afterwards, when all passion has been spent, the historian often sees that it was a conflict between one half that was perhaps too willful and another, half-right, that was perhaps too proud; and behind even this he discovers that it was a terrible predicament which had the effect of putting men at cross-purposes with one another."

He may still question the soundness of Southern leadership; but he will remember that men, whose opportunity in the modern world was one of producing its raw cotton, did not deliberately choose to do so on plantations with Negro slavery. They only went on with what was already at hand in their hurry to prosper. And having done so without the necessity of altering to any degree their social-economic patterns, they saw no reason for changing their traditional notions of the federal character of the national government, the benefits of Negro slavery, or the superiority of a rural-agricultural way of life. The social-intellectual side of the nineteenth century had not come their way. As a result, they were sometimes confused; sometimes reduced to rationalizing; sometimes overwhelmed by guilt.

Nor should the historian give too much moral credit to Northern men, upon whom had been showered all the benefits of the advancing urban-industrial age, for advocating consolidated nationalism, free labor, and democratic-humanitarian reforms. These were the social-intellectual approaches which the new age demanded of those who shared its benefits. Northern men did not in all cases deliberately choose them. They merely accepted them as part of what they were soon calling "Progress."

And so the historian, having heard both sides, begins to understand the "fundamental human predicament . . . which would have led to a serious conflict of wills even if all men had been fairly intelligent and reasonably well-intended." He may, in historical perspective, even "learn to be a little more sorry for both parties" who came to believe that they had no alternative to war. Even the war itself might lose some of its romance, cease to be simply a struggle between good men and bad men, and begin to take on its true meaning as a nation's greatest tragedy. Yet, with all this later day understanding, no historian can ignore the fact that the Southern resort to secession for the protection of slavery reduced the whole matter, for Northern men of that day, to one of saving the Union and destroying slavery as an obligation to the age in which they lived.

Comment on

WHY THE SOUTHERN STATES SECEDED

Charles G. Sellers, Jr.

Professor Craven referred in concluding [his address] to the "terrifying prospect of being labeled 'a revisionist.' "[1] While it is true that the group of Civil War historians called revisionists have differed widely among themselves on particular points, it is also true that they have shared a distinctive emphasis which has become a major element in our thinking about the subject. As one of the most distinguished members of this group, as one of the most influential instructors of a whole generation of historians, Professor Craven has himself become a legitimate subject for historical analysis.

What I want to suggest is that Professor Craven should wear the label "revisionist" proudly. The great and permanent contribution of the revisionists has been their insistence on the centrality of emotion and irrationality (or a-rationality) in the coming

[1] EDITOR's NOTE. After the original papers and critiques were read at the conference, Professor Craven slightly revised his paper. He did not alter his basic theme, but he made some additions (illustrative material principally) and certain changes in phraseology. Thus, in places indicated by footnotes supplied by the editor, the language which Professor Sellers quotes in his critique no longer corresponds precisely to that appearing in Professor Craven's article as printed.

The unrevised version of Professor Craven's paper did not include section 11, he concluded his paper with this statement: "So in conclusion, at the terrifying prospect of being labeled 'a revisionist,' I would like to suggest that the much sought for 'central theme of Southern history' is, and always has been, a proud reluctance to being pushed into the modern world."

of the Civil War. Mary Scrugham first raised the revisionist banner over forty years ago (in *The Peaceable Americans,* 1921) by asserting that "psychological explanations" were fundamental. Drawing on the pioneering works in the infant discipline of social psychology—Graham Wallas, *Human Nature;* Gustave Le Bon, *The Crowd;* William McDougall, *Social Psychology;* and Edward L. Thorndike, *Educational Psychology*—she suggested the applicability to Civil War historiography of such concepts as "the instinct of counter-attack," "the law of the mental unity of crowds," and "the suggestible state of mind."

While subsequent revisionists followed Miss Scrugham's lead in emphasizing emotion—in this, if little else, they were united—the impulse of revisionism was diverted into unprofitable channels. The primitive state of social psychology gave little encouragement to historians who might have wished to press deeper their analysis of the nature, causes, and dynamics of the emotional states that were so evidently important. Also the emotions of the historians themselves were still entangled in the enduring configurations of sectionalism, racism, and egalitarianism that the Civil War so powerfully symbolized. As a result revisionist historiography became preoccupied with questions which were emotionally important to the historians concerned but which impeded a more searching analysis of the emotional states that preceded the Civil War. Was the war repressible or irrepressible? Was slavery on its way to extinction peaceably? Which side was most to blame?

Since the late 1940's revisionism has been under attack. Implicitly or explicitly the critics charge that the revisionists were so horrified by the idea of war, or so intent on exonerating the South, or so insensitive to the moral enormity of slavery that they palliated the South's peculiar institution and aggressive actions, painted the abolitionists as self-righteous fanatics, and blamed irresponsible and/or fanatical leaders, mainly those of an abolitionist stripe, for precipitating a needless war. Under this mounting barrage of criticism revisionism's central insight is in danger of being lost.

Professor Craven rightly protests against the revisionist label if it carries with it this blanket indictment. Certainly he has always given great weight to the moral force of anti-slavery sentiment, and certainly he has recognized that the South as well as the North had its radical agitators. Yet his earlier and most influential writings do reflect some of the revisionist emphases that have been most justly criticized, especially the suggestion that the emotionality of the Civil War generation was somehow needless and artificially generated by irresponsible leaders. In *The Coming of the Civil War* (1942) he wrote:

Stripped of false assumptions, the tragedy of the nation in bloody strife from 1861–1865 must, in large part, be charged to a generation of well-meaning Americans, who, busy with the task of getting ahead, permitted their short-sighted politicians, their over-zealous editors, and their pious reformers to emotionalize real and potential differences and to conjure up distorted impressions of those who dwelt in other parts of the nation. For more than two decades, these molders of public opinion steadily . . . exalted a faltering and decadent labor system, on the one hand, into the cornerstone of a perfect society, and, on the other, into an aggressive, expanding evil about to destroy the white man's heritage and to ruin God's experiment in Democracy. They awakened new fears and led men to hate. . . .

The process by which a repressible conflict was made into an irrepressible one was closely seen and described by a thoughtful Georgia editor in 1858. . . .

In 1861 the crisis which this editor feared was reached. The legal election of a President set two peoples, who knew little of each other as realities, at each other's throats. . . . The cost was more than five billion dollars and more than a half million human lives. When the struggle was over few problems had been solved, and a whole series of new ones had been created far more vexing than those which led to war. Later historians would talk about "a blundering generation."

I have dealt at some length with revisionism and with Professor Craven's earlier views because his paper today has presented a substantially different interpretation. Instead of hearing about "a blundering generation" who "permitted their short-sighted politicians, their over-zealous editors, and their pious reformers to . . . conjure up distorted impressions of those who dwelt in other parts of the nation," we are now told that "the Northern mind and conscience had kept pace with the industry, the cities, the finance, and the railroads of the onrushing nineteenth century," and that "a realization of the dignity of a human being and a deep feeling of guilt for its violation was as marked as the material changes."

In place of "a blundering generation" we now have a "blundering Southern leadership" reinforcing the North's pervasive and ineluctable hostility to slavery. In their "blindness or indifference to the nationalistic and democratic-humanitarian character of the age," John C. Calhoun and his allies "created the impression that there was a 'slave power' bent on spreading its peculiar institution by every means possible to every corner of the nation. . . . By not understanding the fact that they were fighting an age, not just a group of fanatics, they had alarmed and aroused the whole North."

Yet Professor Craven's focus is no longer on an irresponsible leadership in the South any more than in the North. Instead he now squarely asks the question that revisionists have been criticized for avoiding: why did the Civil War generation produce and respond to this kind of leadership? "It is, indeed, difficult to believe that under normal conditions any considerable number of Southerners would have accepted" the oversimplifications of the radical fire-eaters, he tells us. "But nothing, in the 1850's could long remain normal." Northern antislavery sentiment, "when combined with the brutal fact that the South . . . had become a permanent political minority, its social system under moral condemnation by the whole Western world, its economic life . . . reduced to colonial dependence," created "the apprehensions, the fears, the indignation, and the abused[2] self-respect to which the fanatics could appeal. . . . Had not the struggle between the sections at bottom rested on such foundations as these," Professor Craven concludes, "there might have been some way out." Presumably the conflict was inherently irrepressible.

The real focus of Professor Craven's paper is on these Southern apprehensions and fears, on this Southern indignation and abused self-respect, as the fundamental precipitating factors in the coming of war. He recognizes that the problem is not as simple as it may first appear. The seceding South's outcries against Northern aggression on slavery leave much to be explained, he observes. The complaints were suspiciously unspecific; and "Lincoln's oft-repeated statement that he would not interfere with slavery in the

2 EDITOR'S NOTE. The word "abused" is omitted in Professor Craven's revised version.

states where it existed, and the fact that both Congress and the Court would be against him if he should try to do so, only add to the difficulty." Yet there can be no doubt that the Southern feelings of outrage were widespread and genuine. "The only questions," Professor Craven says, "have to do with the reasons for them, and the soundness of those reasons." [3]

By focusing his attention on the Southern feelings that precip-

3 EDITOR'S NOTE. Professor Craven in the unrevised version, following a discussion of statements made in the Southern secession conventions (see p. 62), included the following passage: "The constant reference to 'continued aggression' and the seeming admission that harsh criticism of slavery and the political triumph of the critics had produced the present crisis, leaves much to be explained. Lincoln's oft-repeated statement that he would not interfere with slavery in the states where it existed, and the fact that both Congress and the Court would be against him if he should try to do so, only adds to the difficulty. In fact, the calm assurance that everybody knew all about the wrongs inflicted and the rights denied, creates for the historian, his first problem.

"Where one might reasonably expect to find a long list of the wrongs done or, at least, clear-cut evidence of willful aggression, he finds largely vague generalizations regarding assumed damages and much of dangers anticipated. There is abundant evidence of anger, of hurt pride, and of genuine fear. But in the main, the impression given is that of a feeling of helplessness in the face of what seemed to be a driving force against which resistance had all along been hopeless. Northern men, for some mistaken reason, would not leave the institution of slavery alone. Neither reason nor law seemed to make any difference. Driven by some mysterious force, the tide rolled on. As one frightened editor said, Southerners saw in the 'tremendous popular majorities' which had made Lincoln President, 'the huge mountainous waves that were beating down on the South with resistless force' and that 'must engulf the whole social system of the South in the relentless waters of anti-slavery fanaticism. . . . Whether these apprehensions be well or ill founded,' he added, 'is now of small practical consequence. They sufficiently possess the minds of a majority of the people in several Southern states to render a dissolution of the Union inevitable.'

"The first step, therefore, to be taken in answering the question of why the Southern states seceded, is to recognize the existence of this widespread and generally accepted belief in 'the volumes of insult and the long catalogue of aggressions that have been perpetrated by the North upon the South,' and which it 'would be an insult to the intelligence of the Southern mind to doubt . . . existed.' Even conservative Southerners, by 1860–61, generally agreed that their section 'had been wronged, insulted, injured, and degraded from her equality in the Union.' That their feelings were genuine cannot be doubted. The only questions have to do with the reasons for them and the soundness of those reasons."

Professor Craven replaced this passage by material in paragraphs two and four of section 2 and by sections 3 and 4 of the revised paper.

itated secession and war, by recognizing that those feelings were
not an altogether rational adjustment to reality, and by proposing
to explore the reasons for those feelings, Professor Craven brings
revisionist historiography out of its forty years of wandering in
the wilderness of "needless war" polemics and back to the task
which Mary Scrugham set for it in 1921, the task of analyzing the
psychological dimensions of the sectional conflict.

Professor Craven's paper provides ample materials for such
an analysis. He cites much evidence indicating that the South
reacted mainly to the North's moral condemnation of slavery and
that the South increasingly insisted on national policies that constituted an endorsement of the peculiar institution. Slavery "could
not stand criticism on moral grounds," he remarks early in his
paper. "Secession was an admission of that fact." [4] And near the
end he emphasizes the "curious psychopathic twist" of Yancey
in demanding that Northern Democrats at the Charleston convention endorse slavery as a positive good.

Yet Professor Craven does not draw the indicated conclusions,
and his analysis remains blurred. Partly this is because he has
brought along some baggage from revisionism's forty years of
wandering in the wilderness: a continuing preoccupation with the
economic inefficiency of slavery and with the colonial economic
status of the South. Ignoring the unprecedented prosperity and
entrepreneurial ebullience of the South in the 1850's and the extent
to which the South participated in the spirit of "the onrushing
nineteenth century," Professor Craven takes refuge in the vague
generalization "that the much sought for 'central theme of Southern
history' is, and always has been, a proud reluctance to being
pushed into the modern world." [5]

4 EDITOR'S NOTE. The unrevised version, following quotations from two
Southern editors (see p. 61), contained this passage: "What both [editors]
were saying was that the plantation, as the Southern expression of large-
scale production in a competitive capitalistic society, had become dependent
on Negro slave labor regardless of the inefficiency of the individual worker.
Mass production could subsist on less than maximum individual returns.
The whole Southern economy had been built on such an understanding. And
slavery, as a vital factor in this fragile, undiversified economy, could not
stand criticism on moral grounds. Secession was an admission of that
fact."
5 EDITOR'S NOTE. See above, Editor's Note 1, p. 80.

I would suggest that a more logical product of Professor Craven's evidence and arguments—a more logical conclusion from the profound central insight of revisionist historiography—would be a psychologically sophisticated version of the old "aggressive slavocracy" interpretation of the Civil War. In the same year that Mary Scrugham called for a psychological interpretation of the Civil War, Chauncey S. Boucher published an important article, *"In re* That Aggressive Slavocracy," which satisfactorily demolished the idea of a "slave power conspiracy." In the process, however, Boucher observed that many Southerners "took a stand which may perhaps best be termed 'aggressively defensive' "; and he suggested that this behavior was connected with the fact that when Southerners talked of slavery as a divinely ordained institution, they were in the position of "saying a thing and being conscious while saying it that the thing is not true." Professor Craven similarly observes that the South's psychological environment in the 1850's gave the Southern radicals "the opportunity to shift the Southern efforts from defense to aggression"; and that "they proclaimed the perfection of their own Southern ways and values so intensely as to half convince themselves of the truth of what they were saying." [6]

In evaluating the "aggressively defensive" behavior of the South, it is important to recognize that in the 1850's the South was not only in the midst of the greatest economic boom it had ever experienced but also enjoyed the greatest actual power in the federal government it had ever experienced. Dominating the only national political party and utilizing Northern Democratic politicians who competed with each other in serving Southern wishes as far as they could without being defeated at home, the South controlled the presidency, the Congress, and the Supreme Court. It was under these circumstances of unparalleled prosperity and unparalleled power that the South behaved like a more and more

6 EDITOR'S NOTE. Professor Craven in his revision changed the ending of the sentence (see p. 75). The unrevised version reads: "Closing their eyes to the tattered realities about them, and their minds to all the democratic-humanitarian demands of the age in which they lived, they proclaimed the perfection of their own Southern ways and values so intensely as to half convince themselves of the truth of what they were saying."

aggressive slavocracy, constantly demanding greater and greater reassurances about slavery, especially with reference to the status of slavery in the territories.

In 1820 the South had been willing to accept the principle that Congress should decide the status of slavery in the Louisiana Purchase, provided that some of the territories were reserved for slavery. When the Mexican Cession reopened the question in 1848, the doughface Democratic presidential candidate, Lewis Cass, appealed for Southern support with the doctrine of squatter sovereignty, potentially opening all the new territories to slavery. Then in 1854 Southerners demanded, in the Kansas-Nebraska bill, that Congress go back and apply squatter sovereignty to those territories in the Louisiana Purchase previously reserved as free soil. Roy Nichols' article on "A Century of Kansas-Nebraska Historiography," published in 1954, gave powerful support to the "aggressive slavocracy" thesis by showing that the impetus for repeal of the Missouri Compromise came not from Stephen A. Douglas but from the "F Street mess" of radical Southerners who dominated the Senate and the Pierce administration. By this time Southerners were no longer satisfied with "squatter sovereignty" as applied by territorial legislatures and were insisting on "popular sovereignty," a version of the doctrine that allowed slavery throughout the territorial stage and permitted a decision about its future only at the time of statehood. And when it came to applying "popular sovereignty" to Kansas, Southerners tried to force acceptance of the proslavery constitution drafted by the notoriously unrepresentative Lecompton convention. Then came the Dred Scott decision, buttressing the South's right to take its slaves into any territory and also reasonably raising in Northern minds the spectre of a future decision forcing slaves into the free states. Finally when Stephen A. Douglas—who was willing to be a doughface but who had to be reelected by an alarmed Northern constituency—desperately told Illinois voters that a territorial legislature could keep slavery out by merely refusing to enact police legislation supporting the institution, a considerable segment of the South's leadership demanded enactment of a congressional slave code for the territories.

What is curious about these increasingly aggressive demands

is that they called into existence in the North, as Professor Craven seems to recognize, the powerful free-soil sentiment and the Republican party that were ultimately to destroy the institution the South thought it was defending. What is even more curious is the fact that the South followed this suicidal course with regard to territories when there is little evidence that any substantial number of Southerners ever wanted to carry any actual slaves into any of the territories in question. Some of the most radical Southerners admitted that "slavery by the laws of climate could never take foot-hold in Kansas," and that a proslavery constitution in Kansas, where a majority opposed slavery, "is not worth to the South the paper it is written on." But in the same breath these men demanded the technical right to take slaves to Kansas, because "a just deference to the sensitive honour of the Southern people demanded that there should be at least a *distinct theoretical* recognition of her constitutional rights etc." As a South Carolinian put it, the fight for Kansas involved "a 'point of honor' merely."

It seems to me that the whole pattern of "aggressively defensive" Southern behavior was a series of constantly mounting demands for symbolic acts by which the North would say that slavery was all right. Professor Craven has referred to numerous instances of this kind of behavior. Calhoun's "fatal Southern orthodox platform" of 1837 objected to any Northern meddling with slavery, "under any pretext whatever, political, moral or religious," on the ground, first, that it would be "an assumption of superiority," second, that it would be "insulting to the States interfered with," and only finally that it would tend "to endanger their domestic peace and tranquility." Professor Craven also reminds us of Calhoun's "next equally rash and shortsighted move" of linking the issue of Texas annexation with slavery, in effect saying to Northern Senators, "You can vote for Texas annexation only if you will vote for it as a slavery measure. You can have Texas if you will say that slavery is all right." When the South demands as part of the Compromise of 1850 a stringent Fugitive Slave Act, Professor Craven observes that "nothing could have contributed more towards rendering slavery obnoxious." It is suggestive of the fundamental Southern motivation that this act was drawn in such a way as to involve Northern private citizens in the return of runaway slaves, and that strict Northern compliance with the act was made the condition for continuing Southern acceptance of the Compromise. Professor Craven emphasizes the fact that the North's refusal to comply with the Fugitive Slave Act of 1850 was almost the only evidence Southerners could offer of the Northern aggression they complained about. And yet he quotes that bellwether of Southern radicalism, the Charleston *Mercury,* as saying that nonenforcement of the Fugitive Slave Law was "not of the slightest consequence" as a practical matter. Northern refusals to enforce the act, said the *Mercury,* mattered only "in the insult they conveyed to the South, and the evidence they offered of Northern faithlessness."

These constant demands for symbolic Northern approval of slavery—made all the more strenuously as Southerners succeeded in provoking greater Northern alarm at the encroachments of an "aggressive slavocracy"—suggest that the South was acting irrationally because of the mounting strain of being part of "the onrushing nineteenth century" while trying to maintain an institution condemned by nineteenth-century attitudes which the South fully shared. "The South has been moved to resistance," declared a New Orleans editor on the eve of secession, "chiefly . . . by the popular dogma in the free states that slavery is a crime in the sight of GOD. The South in the eyes of the North, is degraded and unworthy, because of the institution of servitude."

The South did not close its eyes to the nineteenth century; it did not display "a proud reluctance to being pushed into the modern world." [7] It was already so much a part of that world, already so fearful that it was "degraded and unworthy because of the institution of servitude," that it became stridently aggressive, multiplying the threatening forces of outside criticism until the tension became intolerable and finally allowing itself to be swept by its radical leaders into the catharsis of secession and war.

7   EDITOR'S NOTE. See above, Editor's Note 1, p. 80.

IV

WHY THE REPUBLICANS REJECTED BOTH COMPROMISE AND SECESSION

David M. Potter

Historians have a habit of explaining the important decisions of the past in terms of principles. On this basis, it is easy to say that the Republicans rejected compromise because they were committed to the principle of antislavery and that they rejected secession because they were committed to the principle of union. But in the realities of the historical past, principles frequently come into conflict with other principles, and those who make decisions have to choose which principle shall take precedence. When principles thus conflict, as they frequently do, it is meaningless to show merely that a person or a group favors a given principle: the operative question is what priority they give to it. For instance, before the secession crisis arose, there were many Northerners who believed in both the principle of antislavery and the principle of union, but who differed in the priority which they would give to one or the other: William Lloyd Garrison gave the priority to antislavery and proclaimed that there should be "no union with slaveholders." Abraham Lincoln gave, or seemed to give, the priority to union and during the war wrote the famous letter to Horace Greeley in which he said: "My paramount object is to save the Union and it is not either to save or to destroy slavery. What I do about slavery and the colored race, I do because I believe it helps to save the Union, and what I forbear, I forbear because I do not believe it would help to save the Union." Lincoln was always precise to almost a unique degree in his statements, and it is interesting to note that he did not say that it was not his object to destroy slavery; what he said was that it was not his paramount object—he did not give it the highest priority.

To state this point in another way, if we made an analysis of the moderate Republicans and of the abolitionists solely in terms of their principles, we would hardly be able to distinguish between them, for both were committed to the principle of antislavery and to the principle of union. It was the diversity in the priorities which they gave to these two principles that made them distinctive from each other.

A recognition of the priorities, therefore, may in many cases serve a historian better than a recognition of principles. But while it is important to recognize which principle is, as Lincoln expressed it, paramount, it is no less important to take account of the fact that men do not like to sacrifice one principle for the sake of another and do not even like to recognize that a given situation may require a painful choice between principles. Thus, most Northern antislavery men wanted to solve the slavery question within the framework of union, rather than to reject the Union because it condoned slavery; correspondingly, most Northern Unionists wanted to save the Union while taking steps against slavery, rather than by closing their eyes to the slavery question.

In short, this means—and one could state it almost as an axiom —that men have a tendency to believe that their principles can be reconciled with one another, and that this belief is so strong that it inhibits their recognition of realistic alternatives in cases where the alternatives would involve a choice between cherished principles. This attitude has been clearly defined in the homely phrase that we all like to have our cake and eat it too.

Perhaps all this preliminary consideration of theory seems excessively abstract and you will feel that I ought to get on to the Republicans, the crisis, and the rejection of compromise and secession; but before I do, let me take one more step with my theory. If the participants in a historical situation tend to see the alternatives in that situation as less clear, less sharply focused than they really are, historians probably tend to see the alternatives as more clear, more evident, more sharply focused than they really were. We see the alternatives as clear because we have what we foolishly believe to be the advantage of hindsight—which is really a disadvantage in understanding how a situation seemed to the participants. We know, in short, that the Republicans did reject both compromise and secession (I will return to the details of this rejection later) and that the four-year conflict known as the Civil War eventuated. We therefore tend to think not only that conflict of some kind was the alternative to the acceptance of compromise or the acquiescence in secession, but actually that this particular war—with all its costs, its sacrifices, and its consequences—was the alternative. When men choose a course of action which had a given result, historians will tend to attribute to them not only the choice of the course, but even the choice of the result. Yet one needs only to state this tendency clearly in order to demonstrate the fallacy in it. Whatever choice anyone exercised in 1860–61, no one chose the American Civil War, because it lay behind the veil of the future; it did not exist as a choice.

Hindsight not only enables historians to define the alternatives in the deceptively clear terms of later events; it also gives them a deceptively clear criterion for evaluating the alternatives, which is in terms of later results. That is, we now know that the war did result in the preservation of the Union and in the abolition of chattel slavery. Accordingly, it is easy, with hindsight, to attribute to the participants not only a decision to accept the alternative of a war whose magnitude they could not know, but also to credit them with choosing results which they could not foresee. The war, as it developed, certainly might have ended in the quicker defeat of the Southern movement, in which case emancipation would apparently not have resulted; or it might have ended in the independence of of the Southern Confederacy, in which case the Monday morning quarterbacks of the historical profession would have been in the position of saying that the rash choice of a violent and coercive course had destroyed the possibility of a harmonious, voluntary restoration of the Union—a restoration of the kind which William H. Seward was trying to bring about.

I suppose all this is only equivalent to saying that the supreme task of the historian, and the one of most superlative difficulty, is to see the past through the imperfect eyes of those who lived it and not with his own omniscient twenty-twenty vision. I am not suggesting that any of us can really do this, but only that it is what we must attempt.

What do we mean, specifically, by saying that the Republican party rejected compromise? Certain facts are reasonably familiar in this connection, and may be briefly recalled. In December, 1860, at the time when a number of secession conventions had been called in the Southern states but before any ordinances of secession had been adopted, various political leaders brought forward proposals to give assurances to the Southerners. The most prominent of these was the plan by Senator John J. Crittenden of Kentucky to place an amendment in the Constitution which would restore and extend the former Missouri Compromise line of 36° 30', prohibiting slavery in Federal territory north of the line and sanctioning it south of the line. In a Senate committee, this proposal was defeated with five Republicans voting against it and none in favor of it, while the non-Republicans favored it six to two. On January 16, after four states had adopted ordinances of secession, an effort was made to get the Crittenden measure out of committee and on to the floor of the Senate. This effort was defeated by 25 votes against to 23 in favor. This was done on a strict party vote, all 25 of the votes to defeat being cast by Republicans. None of those in favor were Republicans. On March 2, after the secession of the lower South was complete, the Crittenden proposal was permitted to come to a vote. In the Senate, it was defeated 19 to 20. All 20 of the negative votes were Republican, not one of the affirmative votes was so. In the House, it was defeated 80 to 113. Not one of the 80 was a Republican, but 110 of the 113 were Republicans.

Another significant measure of the secession winter was a proposal to amend the Constitution to guarantee the institution of slavery in the states. This proposed amendment—ironically designated by the same number as the one which later freed the slaves —was actually adopted by Congress, in the House by a vote of 128 to 65, but with 44 Republicans in favor and 62 opposed; in the Senate by a vote of 24 to 12, but with 8 Republicans in favor and 12 opposed.

While opposing these measures, certain Republicans, including

Charles Francis Adams, brought forward a bill to admit New Mexico to statehood without restrictions on slavery, and they regarded this as a compromise proposal. But this measure was tabled in the House, 115 to 71, with Republicans casting 76 votes to table and 26 to keep the bill alive. Thus, it can be said, without qualification, that between December and March, no piece of compromise legislation was ever supported by a majority of Republican votes, either in the Senate or the House, either in committee or on the floor. This, of course, does not mean either that they ought to have supported the measures in question, or that such measures would have satisfied the Southern states. It is my own belief that the balance between the secessionist and the non-secessionist forces was fairly close in all of the seceding states except South Carolina, and that the support of Congress for a compromise would have been enough to tip the balance. But the Crittenden measure would possibly have opened the way for Southern filibustering activities to enlarge the territorial area south of 36° 30′ —at least this was apparently what Lincoln feared—and the "thirteenth" amendment would have saddled the country with slavery more or less permanently. When we say, then, that the Republicans rejected compromise, we should take care to mean no more than we say. They did, by their votes, cause the defeat of measures which would otherwise have been adopted by Congress, which were intended and generally regarded as compromise measures. In this sense, they rejected compromise.

When we say the Republican party rejected secession, the case is so clear that it hardly needs a recital of proof. It is true that at one stage of the crisis, many Republicans did talk about letting the slave states go. Horace Greeley wrote his famous, ambiguous, oft-quoted, and much misunderstood editorial saying that "if the cotton states shall become satisfied that they can do better out of the Union than in it, we insist on letting them go in peace." Later, when the situation at Fort Sumter had reached its highest tension, a number of Republicans, including Salmon P. Chase, Simon Cameron, Gideon Welles, and Caleb Smith, all in the cabinet, advised Lincoln to evacuate the fort rather than precipitate hostilities; but this hardly means that they would not have made the issue of union in some other way. Lincoln himself definitively rejected secession in his inaugural address when he declared: "No state upon its own mere motion, can lawfully get out of the Union. . . . I . . . consider that in view of the Constitution and the laws, the Union is unbroken; and to the extent of my ability I shall take care, as the Constitution itself expressly enjoins upon me, that the laws of the Union be faithfully executed in all the States." After the fall of Fort Sumter, he translated this affirmation into action by calling for 75,000 volunteers, and by preparing to use large-scale military measures to hold the South in the Union. The fact that no major figure in the North, either Republican or Democrat, ever proposed to acquiesce in the rending of the Union and that no proposal to do so was ever seriously advocated or voted upon in Congress, is evidence enough that the Republicans rejected secession even more decisively than they rejected compromise. They scarcely even felt the need to consider the question or to make an organized presentation of their reasons. It is true that some of them said that they would rather have disunion than compromise, but this was a way of saying how much they objected to compromise, and not how little they objected to separation. It was almost exactly equivalent to the expression, "Death rather than dishonor," which has never been understood to mean an acceptance of death, but rather an adamant rejection of dishonor.

Here, then, in briefest outline is the record of the Republican rejection of compromise and of secession. What we are concerned with, however, is not the mere fact of the rejection, but rather with its meaning. Why did the Republicans do this? What was their motivation? What did they think would follow from their decision? What did they believe the alternatives to be? Specifically, did this mean that the choice as they saw it was clear-cut, and that they conceived of themselves as opting in favor of war in a situation where they had a choice between secession and war? As I come to this question, I must revert to my comments earlier in this paper by pointing out again the tendency of historians to see the alternatives with preternatural clarity and the fallacy involved in attributing to the participants a capacity to define the alternatives in the same crystalline terms.

Peace or war? Compromise or conflict? Separation or coercion?

These alternatives have such a plausible neatness, such a readiness in fitting the historian's pigeon holes, that it is vastly tempting to believe that they define the choices which people were actually making and not just the choices that we think they ought to have been making. We all know, today, that economists once fell into fallacies by postulating an economic man who behaved economically in the way economists thought he ought to behave. But even though we do know this, we are not as wary as we should be of the concept of what might be called an historical man who behaved historically in the way historians thought he ought to have behaved. It is very well for us, a hundred years later, to analyze the record and to say there were three alternatives, as distinct as the three sides of a triangle, namely compromise, voluntary separation, or war. Indeed this analysis may be correct. The error is not in our seeing it this way, but in our supposing that since we do see it in this way, the participants must have seen it in this way also.

Nothing can be more difficult—indeed impossible—than to reconstruct how a complex situation appeared to a varied lot of people, not one of whom saw or felt things in exactly the same way as any other one, a full century ago. But in the effort to approximate these realities as far as we can, it might be useful to begin by asking to what extent the choices of compromise, separation, or war had emerged as the possible alternatives in the minds of the citizens as they faced the crisis. Did they see the Crittenden proposals as embodying a possibility for compromise, and did a vote against these proposals mean an acceptance of the alternatives of war or separation? Did a policy which rejected both compromise and war indicate an acceptance of the alternative of voluntary separation? Did a decision to send food to Sumter and to keep the flag flying mean an acceptance of war? By hindsight, all of these indications appear plausible, and yet on close scrutiny, it may appear that not one of them is tenable in an unqualified way.

Did a vote against the Crittenden proposals indicate a rejection of the possibility of compromise? If Republicans voted against the Crittenden proposals, did this mean that they saw themselves as rejecting the principle of compromise and that they saw the possibilities thereby narrowed to a choice between voluntary separation or fierce, coercive war? If they repelled the idea of voluntary separation, did this imply that they were prepared to face a choice between political compromise or military coercion as the only means of saving the Union? If they urged the administration to send food to the besieged men in Sumter and to keep the flag flying there, did this mean that they had actually accepted the irrepressibility of the irrepressible conflict, and that they regarded peaceable alternatives as exhausted?

Although it makes the task of our analysis considerably more complex to say so, still it behooves us to face the music of confusion and to admit that not one of these acts was necessarily seen by the participants as narrowing the alternatives in the way which our after-the-fact analysis might indicate. To see the force of this reality, it is necessary to look at each of these contingencies in turn.

First, there is the case of those Republicans, including virtually all the Republican members in the Senate or the House, who refused to support the Crittenden proposals. To be sure, these men were accused of sacrificing the Union or of a callous indifference to the hazard of war; and to be sure, there were apparently some men like Zachariah Chandler who actually wanted war. (It was Chandler, you will recall, who said, "Without a little blood-letting, the Union will not be worth a rush.") But there were many who had grown to entertain sincere doubts as to whether the adoption of the Crittenden proposals, or the grant of any other concessions to the South, would actually bring permanent security to the Union. The danger to the Union lay, as they saw it, in the fact that powerful groups in many Southern states believed that any state had an unlimited right to withdraw from the Union and thus disrupt it. Southerners had fallen into the habit of asserting this right whenever they were much dissatisfied and declaring they would exercise it if their demands were not met. They had made such declarations between 1846 and 1850, when the Free-Soilers proposed to exclude slavery from the Mexican Cession. They had done so again in 1850 when they wanted a more stringent fugitive slave law. The threat of secession had been heard once more in 1856 when it appeared that the Republicans might elect a Free-Soiler to the presidency. On each occasion, concessions had been made: the

Compromise of 1850 made it legally possible to take slaves to New Mexico; the Compromise also gave the slave owners a fugitive act that was too drastic for their own good; in 1856, timid Union-loving Whigs rallied to Buchanan and thus helped to avert the crisis that Frémont's election might have brought. Each such concession, of course, confirmed the Southern fire-eaters in their habit of demanding further concessions, and it strengthened their position with their constituents in the South by enabling them to come home at periodic intervals with new tribute that they had extorted from the Yankees. From the standpoint of a sincere Unionist, there was something self-defeating about getting the Union temporarily past a crisis by making concessions which strengthened the disunionist faction and perpetuated the tendency toward periodic crises. This was a point on which Republicans sometimes expressed themselves very emphatically. For instance, Schuyler Colfax, in 1859, wrote to his mother about conditions in Congress: "We are still just where we started six months ago," he said, "except that our Southern friends have dissolved the Union forty or fifty times since then." In the same vein, Carl Schurz ridiculed the threat of secession, while campaigning for Lincoln in 1860: "There had been two overt attempts at secession already," Schurz was reported as saying, "one the secession of the Southern students from the medical school at Philadelphia . . . the second upon the election of Speaker Pennington, when the South seceded from Congress, went out, took a drink, and then came back. The third attempt would be," he prophesied, "when Old Abe would be elected. They would then again secede and this time would take two drinks, but would come back again." Schurz's analysis may have been good wit, but of course it was disastrously bad prophesy, and it had the fatal effect of preparing men systematically to misunderstand the signs of danger when these signs appeared. The first signs would be merely the first drink; confirmatory signs would be the second drink. James Buchanan recognized, as early as 1856, that men were beginning to underestimate the danger to the Union simply because it was chronic and they were too familiar with it: "We have so often cried wolf," he said, "that now, when the wolf is at the door it is difficult to make the people believe it." Abraham Lincoln provided a distinguished proof of Buchanan's point in August, 1860, when he wrote: "The people of the South have too much of good sense and good temper to attempt the ruin of the government rather than see it administered as it was administered by the men who made it. At least, so I hope and believe." As usual, Lincoln's statement was a gem of lucidity, even when it was unconsciously so. He hoped and believed. The wish was father to the thought.

The rejection of compromise, then, did not mean an acceptance of separation or war. On the contrary, to men who regarded the threat of secession as a form of political blackmail rather than a genuine indication of danger to the Union, it seemed that danger of disunion could be eliminated only by eliminating the disunionists, and this could never be accomplished by paying them off at regular intervals. The best hope of a peaceful union lay in a development of the strength of Southern Unionists, who would never gain the ascendancy so long as the secessionists could always get what they demanded. Viewed in this light, compromise might be detrimental to the cause of union; and rejection of compromise might be the best way to avoid the dangers of separation or of having to fight the disunionists.

If the rejection of compromise did not mean the acceptance of either separation or war, did the rejection of separation mean an acceptance of a choice between compromise and coercion as the remaining alternatives? This was the choice which history has seemed to indicate as the real option open to the country. But, though the unfolding of events may subsequently have demonstrated that these were the basic alternatives, one of the dominating facts about the Republicans in the winter of 1860–61 is that they rejected the idea of voluntary disunion and also rejected the idea of compromise, without any feeling that this narrowing of the spectrum would lead them to war. At this juncture, what may be called the illusion of the Southern Unionists played a vital part. Both Lincoln and Seward and many another Republican were convinced that secessionism was a superficial phenomenon. They believed that it did not represent the most fundamental impulses of the South, and that although the Southern Unionists had been silenced by the clamor of the secessionists a deep vein of Unionist feeling still survived in the South and could be rallied, once the

Southern people realized that Lincoln was not an Illinois version of William Lloyd Garrison and that the secessionists had been misleading them. Lincoln and Seward became increasingly receptive to this view during the month before Lincoln's inauguration. Between December 20 and March 4, seven Southern states had held conventions, and each of these conventions had adopted an ordinance of secession. But on February 4, the secessionists were defeated in the election for the Virginia convention. Within four weeks thereafter, they were again defeated in Tennessee, where the people refused even to call a convention; in Arkansas, where the secessionist candidates for a state convention were defeated; in Missouri, where the people elected a convention so strongly anti-secessionist that it voted 89 to 1 against disunion; and in North Carolina, where anti-secessionist majorities were elected and it was voted that the convention should not meet.

It clearly looked as though the tide of secession had already turned. Certainly, at the time when Lincoln came to the presidency, the movement for a united South had failed. There were, altogether, fifteen slave states. Seven of these, from South Carolina, along the south Atlantic and Gulf coast to Texas, had seceded; but eight others, including Delaware, Kentucky, and Maryland, as well as the five that I have already named, were still in the Union and clearly intended to remain there. In these circumstances, the New York *Tribune* could speak of the Confederacy as a "heptarchy," and Seward could rejoice, as Henry Adams reported, that "this was only a temporary fever and now it has reached the climax and favorably passed it." The Southern Unionists were already asserting themselves, and faith in them was justified. Thus, on his way east from Springfield, Lincoln stated in a speech at Steubenville, Ohio, that "the devotion to the Constitution is equally great on both sides of the [Ohio] River." From this it seemed to follow that, as he also said on his trip, "there is no crisis but an artificial one. . . . Let it alone and it will go down of itself." Meanwhile, Seward had been saying, ever since December, that the Gulf states would try to secede, but that unless they received the backing of the border states, they would find their petty little combination untenable and would have to come back to the Union. Again we owe to Henry Adams the report that Seward said, "We shall keep the border states, and in three months or thereabouts, if we hold off, the Unionists and the disunionists will have their hands on each others throats in the cotton states."

Today, our hindsight makes it difficult for us to understand this reliance upon Southern Unionism, since most of the unionism which existed was destroyed by the four years of war; and it was never what Seward and Lincoln believed it to be in any case. But it seemed quite real when five slave states in rapid succession decided against secession. Thus, in terms of our alternatives of compromise, separation, or war, it is interesting to see that an editorial in the New York *Tribune* on March 27, 1861, specifically examined the alternatives and specifically said that there were only three; but the three which it named were not the three we tend to perceive today. The fact that this editorial, rather closely resembling one in the New York *Times,* was probably inspired by the administration, gives it additional interest.

The *Tribune* began by saying that there were but three possible ways in which to meet the secession movement. One was "by prompt, resolute, unflinching resistance"—what I have been calling the alternative of war; the second was "by complete acquiescence in . . . secession"—that is, separation. But instead of naming compromise as the third alternative, the *Tribune* numbered as three "a Fabian policy, which concedes nothing, yet employs no force in support of resisted Federal authority, hoping to wear out the insurgent spirit and in due time re-establish the authority of the union in the revolted or seceded states by virtue of the returning sanity and loyalty of their own people." As the editorial continued, it explained the reasoning which lay behind the advocacy of this policy.

To war on the Seceders is to give to their yet vapory institutions the strong cement of blood—is to baptize their nationality in the mingled life-blood of friends and foes. But let them severely alone—allow them to wear out the military ardor of their adherents in fruitless drilling and marches, and to exhaust the patience of their fellow-citizens by the amount and frequency of their pecuniary exactions—and the fabric of their power will melt away like fog in the beams of a morning sun. Only give them rope, and they will speedily fulfill their destiny—the People, even of South Carolina, rejecting their sway as intolerable, and returning to the mild and paternal guardianship of the Union.

In behalf of this policy, it is urged that the Secessionists are a minority even in the seceded States; that they have grasped power by usurpation and retain it by terrorism; that they never dare submit the question of Union or Disunion fairly and squarely to the people, and always shun a popular vote when they can. In view of these facts, the Unionists of the South urge that the Government shall carry forebearance to the utmost, in the hope that the Nullifiers will soon be overwhelmed by the public sentiment of their own section, and driven with ignominy from power.

It seems reasonably clear that this editorial defined quite accurately the plan of action which Lincoln had announced in his inaugural. In that address, although affirming in general terms a claim of federal authority which, as the *Tribune* expressed it, conceded nothing, he made it quite clear that he would, as the *Tribune* also said, "employ no force" in the immediate situation. He specifically said he would not use force to deliver the mails—they would only be delivered unless repelled. He specifically said that federal marshals and judges would not be sent into areas where these functions had been vacated. "While the strict legal right may exist in the government to enforce the exercise of these offices, the attempt to do so would be so irritating that I deem it better to forego for the time the use of such offices." Without officials for enforcement, Lincoln's statement that he would uphold the law became purely a declaration of principle, with no operative or functional meaning. Finally, after having first written into his inaugural a statement that "all the power at my disposal will be used to reclaim the public property and places which have fallen," he struck this passage from the address as it was ultimately delivered. It was at about this time that Senator William P. Fessenden of Maine wrote that "Mr. Lincoln believed that gentleness and a conciliatory policy would prevent secession"—as if secession had not already occurred.

Finally, there is a question of whether even the decision to send supplies to Fort Sumter involved a clear acceptance of the alternative of war as well as a rejection of the alternatives of separation or compromise. Professor Stampp and Richard Current have both argued with considerable persuasiveness that Lincoln must have known that the Sumter expedition would bring war, since his informants from Charleston had warned him that such an expedition would be met with military force; and they have shown too that anyone with as much realism as Lincoln had in his makeup must have recognized that the chances for peace were slipping away. Yet I think their argument is more a reasoning from logic—that Lincoln must have seen the situation as we see it—and not an argument based primarily on expressions by Lincoln himself, showing that he had abandoned his belief in Southern Unionism and accepted the alternative of war. Indeed, insofar as we have expressions from him, he continued to believe in the strength of Southern Unionism. Even when he sent his war message to Congress on July 4, he said: "It may well be questioned whether there is today a majority of the legally qualified voters of any state, except perhaps South Carolina, in favor of disunion. There is much reason to believe that the Union men are in the majority in many, if not in every one of the so-called seceded states."

The crisis at Fort Sumter has possibly had almost too sharp a focus placed upon it by historians, and I do not want to dissect that question all over again in this paper. I will state briefly that, in my opinion, Lincoln pursued the most peaceful course that he believed was possible for him to pursue without openly abandoning the principle of union. That is, he assured the Confederates that food only would be sent into Fort Sumter, and nothing else would be done to strengthen the Union position unless the delivery of the food was resisted. While this may be construed, and has been construed, as a threat to make war if the food were not allowed, it can equally well be regarded as a promise that no reinforcement would be undertaken if the delivery of the food was permitted. Lincoln's critics, who accuse him of a covert policy to begin in an advantageous way a war which he now recognized to be inevitable, have never said what more peaceable course he could have followed that would have been consistent with his purpose to save the Union. Thus, they are in the anomalous position of saying that a man who followed the most peaceable course possible was still, somehow, a maker of war.

But as I suggested a moment ago, this focus upon Fort Sumter can perhaps be intensified too much. Even if Lincoln anticipated that there would be shooting at Sumter (and he must have known that there was a strong likelihood of it), what would this tell us about the choice of alternatives leading to the American Civil War? We may again revert to the somewhat arbitrary practice of answering this question in terms of the alternatives as they appear to us now. If the situation is viewed in this way, one would say we have three options neatly laid in a row: separation, compromise, war. If a man rejects any two of them, he is choosing the third; and since Lincoln and the Republicans rejected separation or compromise, this means that they exercised a choice for war. As a statement of the way in which the historical process narrows the field of possible action, this may be realistic; but for illumination of the behavior of men it seems to me very misleading. It assumes two things: first that choices are positive rather than negative; second that a choice of a course which leads to a particular result is in fact a choice of that result. Neither of these assumptions seems valid. What often happens is not that a given course is chosen because it is acceptable, but that given alternatives are rejected because they are regarded as totally unacceptable; thus one course remains which becomes the course followed, not because it was chosen, but because it was what was left.

When Lincoln ordered the Sumter expedition to sail, it was not because he wanted to do so; it was because he hated even worse the contingency of permitting the Sumter garrison to be starved into surrender. As he himself said, he had been committed to "the exhaustion of peaceful measures, before a resort to any stronger ones." But by mid-April at Sumter, the peaceful measures had all been exhausted; and the course that Lincoln followed was taken not because it was what he had chosen, but because it was what was left. That course resulted, as we now say, in the bombardment of Sumter, and the bombardment of Sumter was followed by four years of fighting which we call the Civil War. But even though the sending of the expedition led to events which in turn led on to war, it does not follow that the choice to send the expedition involved an acceptance of the alternative of war.

If deeds and consequences could be thus equated, our view of human nature would have to be more pessimistic than it is; and at the same time, our view of the future of humanity might perhaps be somewhat more optimistic. For it would imply that men have deliberately caused the succession of wars that have blotted the record of human history—certainly a harsh verdict to pronounce on humanity—and it would also imply that they have a certain measure of choice as to what forces of destruction they will release in the world—a proposition which would be comforting in the age of nuclear fission. But when we examine the situations of the past, how seldom does it appear that men defined the alternatives logically, chose the preferable alternative, and moved forward to the result that was intended? How often, on the other hand, do we find that they grope among the alternatives, avoiding whatever action is most positively or most immediately distasteful, and thus eliminate the alternatives until only one is left—at which point, as Lincoln said, it is necessary to have recourse to it since the other possibilities are exhausted or eliminated. In this sense, when the Republicans rejected both compromise and secession, thus narrowing the range of possibilities to include only the contingency of war, it was perhaps not because they really preferred the Civil War, with all its costs, to separation or to compromise, but because they could see the consequences of voting for compromise or the consequences of accepting separation more readily than they could see the consequences of following the rather indecisive course that ended in the bombardment of Fort Sumter. They did not know that it would end by leaving them with a war on their hands, any more than they knew it would cost the life of one soldier, either Rebel or Yank, for every six slaves who were freed and for every ten white Southerners who were held in the Union. When they rejected compromise, because they could not bear to make concessions to the fire-eaters, and rejected separation, because they could not bear to see the Union broken up, this does not mean that they accepted war or that they were able to bear the cost which this war would make them pay. It may really mean that they chose a course whose consequences they could not see in preference to courses whose consequences were easier to appraise.

Historians try to be rational beings and tend to write about history as if it were a rational process. Accordingly, they number the alternatives, and talk about choices and decisions, and equate decisions with what the decisions led to. But if we examine the record of modern wars, it would seem that the way people get into a war is seldom by choosing it; usually it is by choosing a course that leads to it—which is a different thing altogether. Although war seems terribly decisive, perhaps it requires less positive decision to get into wars than it does to avert them. For one can get into a war without in any way foreseeing it or imagining it, which is easy. But to avert war successfully, it has to be foreseen or imagined, which is quite difficult. If this is true, it means that the Republicans may have rejected separation and compromise not because they accepted the alternative, but precisely because they could not really visualize the alternative. When they took the steps that led them into a war, they did so not because they had decisively chosen the road to Appomattox or even the road to Manassas, in preference to the other paths; instead they did so precisely because they could not grasp the fearfully decisive consequences of the rather indecisive line of action which they followed in the months preceding their fateful rendezvous.

Comment on

WHY THE REPUBLICANS REJECTED BOTH COMPROMISE AND SECESSION

Kenneth M. Stampp

I assume that we are concerned not only with Lincoln and the Republican members of Congress but also with Republican governors, Republican members of the state legislatures, and rank-and-file Republican voters as well. For the vast majority of these Republicans also rejected compromise and secession.

As I see it, Professor Potter's argument runs something like this: (1) Men do not like to think that the principles they cherish may conflict with each other. This prevents them from seeing realistic alternatives when the alternatives force them to choose between their principles. (2) The alternatives are never as clear to the participants in a crisis as they are to historians with their hindsight. The power of hindsight makes it difficult for historians to see a historical situation as the participants saw it. (3) With our hindsight we know that the Republicans rejected compromise and secession and that the result was the Civil War. Therefore, we tend to think the Civil War that actually occurred was the clear alternative to accepting compromise or secession. (4) Hindsight also enables us to judge alternatives in terms of results that participants could never have anticipated. Thus the rejection of compromise and secession led to a four-year war, to the preservation of the Union, and to the abolition of slavery; but no one in the winter of 1860–61 could have known that these would be the results.

Up to this point there is nothing in Professor Potter's argument with which I would disagree, except the conclusion he draws from it as stated here. The "supreme task of the historian," he says, "is to see the past through the imperfect eyes of those who lived it." In my opinion, this is one valid way to see the past; but having accomplished it, the historian's task is but half done. The other way to see the past is with all the wisdom and perspective that experience and hindsight can give us. It was hindsight that enabled Professor Potter to describe Carl Schurz's remarks about the approaching crisis as "disastrously bad prophesy" and to show how Schurz helped to prepare men to "misunderstand the signs of danger." It was hindsight once more that enabled him to discern the element of tragedy in human existence as he did so brilliantly in the last pages of his paper—how men throughout history, without willing it, maneuver themselves into situations that culminate in disaster. We must use hindsight as Professor Potter uses it: not to judge and condemn the men of the past, but to understand *why* their best-laid plans so often went astray.

But for the problem at hand—that is, determining why Republicans rejected compromise and secession—Professor Potter believes that we must see the situation as the participants saw it. He objects, therefore, to describing the alternatives as compromise, peaceful secession, or war, because we can see that these were the alternatives only with hindsight. When the Republicans rejected compromise and peaceful secession, he says, they were not necessarily choosing war. I think Professor Potter is correct in this, but I do not think this is the most fruitful way to consider the alternatives. There is another way that brings the alternatives as the Republicans of 1860–61 saw them much closer to the alternatives as we, with our hindsight, see them now. The alternatives were these: (1) compromise, (2) acquiescence in secession, or (3) *the use of whatever force might be necessary to collect federal revenues and to recover or maintain possession of federal property.* These were the alternatives as most Republicans understood them then, and they were the real alternatives as we know from our hindsight.

But from the perspective of 1861, the consequence of using force against the South to collect the revenues and hold federal property was not *necessarily* war. A few Republicans thought it would be; others feared it might be; but many others hoped it would not be. The use of force might have resulted only in a few minor skirmishes, followed by the quick submission of the Southern rebels. The crisis might have been over in a few weeks. Better still, a sufficient demonstration of federal power might have resulted in the immediate collapse of the Confederacy without so much as a skirmish. Thus Republicans could, as most of them actually did, reject compromise and peaceful secession and choose coercion (they called it "the enforcement of the laws") without favoring war or believing that their choice would lead to war. I do not think that even Zachariah Chandler wanted war. After all, he asked only for "a little blood-letting." I believe that when the alternatives are understood in this way, we have a partial answer to the question of why the Republicans rejected compromise and peaceful secession. Thus, even if Republicans believed that Southerners were serious about secession, they could reject compromise and peaceful secession without feeling that war was the only remaining alternative. A mere show of force might have been enough. This generalization is in agreement with the position Professor Potter takes in the concluding pages of his paper, but not with the position he takes in the middle part.

In the middle part, Professor Potter would say that I have begged the question, for I have presupposed not only that Southerners were serious about breaking up the Union but also that Republicans *knew* they were serious and considered alternatives accordingly. This is a presupposition that Professor Potter will not accept, and this is crucial to his explanation of why the Republicans rejected compromise and peaceful secession.

Many Republicans, he thinks, had come to the conclusion that Southerners had got into a bad habit of threatening to secede whenever they failed to get what they wanted. Therefore, according to Professor Potter, Republicans considered the threat of secession to be a form of political blackmail. To compromise with men such as these would only strengthen the disunion movement and make matters worse. More than that, Professor Potter believes that many Republicans thought secessionism lacked basic strength and that most Southerners were actually Unionists at heart. Given time and encouragement, Southern Unionists would suppress the secessionists and regain control; and the Union would be restored without either compromise or war. Thus the alternatives were not compromise, peaceful secession, or force (as I have suggested that Republicans understood them); rather, the alternatives were compromise, peaceful secession, or a "Fabian policy which concedes nothing, yet employs no force" but depends instead on voluntary reunion "through the returning sanity" of the Southern people. Therefore, Professor Potter suggests that Republicans rejected compromise and peaceful secession because they believed the alternative was not war but a reliance on Southern Unionism. Whether he believes that this was the position of *most* Republicans is not clear. Professor Potter says *many,* and among them he includes Lincoln and Seward.

Assuming this generalization to be true for many Republicans, it is still necessary to explain why those who did *not* rely on Southern Unionism (however many there were) rejected compromise and peaceful secession; and I have suggested that it was because they saw the "enforcement of the laws" as an alternative that would not necessarily lead to war. But at this point I would like to consider the alternative of voluntary reunion which Professor Potter believes many Republicans favored. I think the best way to consider it is to take a look at the Northern Democrats and to note what *they* were saying during the crisis. Most Democrats, like the Republicans, rejected peaceful secession; but, unlike the Republicans, they strongly favored compromise, and almost none of them showed any faith in voluntary reunion. Indeed, they repeatedly warned that the inevitable alternative to compromise was *war*—a long and sanguinary war, from which the country would not recover for decades.

Thus we seem to have many Republicans rejecting compromise and saying hopefully and mistakenly that Southern Unionists would soon suppress the secessionists and restore the Union; and we seem to have the Democrats begging for compromise and making what in retrospect proved to be the most realistic predictions about the consequences of rejecting compromise. Are we to conclude from this that the Democrats were a more perspicacious lot than the Republicans? I think not. Rather, it is much more likely that neither the Republicans nor the Democrats were quite sure what the ultimate consequences of rejecting compromise would be. (This, I believe, is nearly the position that Professor Potter takes in the concluding pages of his paper—a position that he does not entirely reconcile with the one he takes in the middle section.)

Why did the Democrats predict war? I would suggest that their desire to achieve a compromise tempted them to paint the most horrible picture of the consequences of *not* compromising. In short, they were trying to frighten people into accepting a compromise. As for the Republicans, their opposition to compromise tempted them to paint a more cheerful picture of the consequences of not compromising. Voluntary reunion was not so much an alternative as a political strategem used by some Republicans who, as a matter of fact, either did not know what the consequences of rejecting compromise would be or preferred the alternative of enforcing the laws.

This is not to say that there were no Republicans who really believed a Unionist reaction would take place in the South. I think there were some, especially in the early weeks of the crisis before South Carolina seceded and seized Fort Moultrie. After that, the evidence indicates that the number of Republicans who believed in this easy solution dwindled rapidly. To put it another way, a growing number of Republicans—I think the great majority of them by January—began to suspect that the federal government might have to take positive action, that is, enforce the laws, in order to suppress the secessionists. Seward, we know, continued to have faith in voluntary reunion almost to the outbreak of war. But not Lincoln. He seems to have believed in this remedy in November and early December, but there is considerable evidence that he had begun to change his mind when South Carolina seceded.

The evidence is available in Lincoln's collected works. On December 21, he wrote to Francis P. Blair, Sr., that if the forts were surrendered before the inauguration they would have to be retaken afterward. On the same day he wrote to Elihu B. Washburne asking him to tell General Scott "to be as well prepared as he can to either *hold* or *retake* the forts, as the case may require, at, and after the inauguration." On December 22, Lincoln wrote to

Major David Hunter: "If the forts fall, my judgment is that they are to be retaken." On the same day he wrote to Peter Sylvester: "If Mr. B[uchanan] surrenders the forts, I think they must be retaken."

The most revealing of these letters was one, dated December 29, to James Watson Webb, editor of the New York *Courier and Enquirer*. Webb had written to ask Lincoln's views on how to deal with secession, to which Lincoln replied: "I think we should hold the forts, or retake them, as the case may be, and collect the revenue. *We* shall have to forego the use of the federal courts, and *they* that of the mails, for a while. We can not fight them into holding courts, or receiving mails. This is an outline of my view; and perhaps suggests sufficiently the whole of it." There is here not a hint of voluntary reunion as a way of dealing with the crisis; and I am inclined to agree with Professor Potter that "Lincoln was always precise to a unique degree in his statements."

Actually, Lincoln, in his letter to Webb, outlined precisely the policy he described in more detail in his inaugural address. This was the policy he believed in from late December until March 4; and I think it is the policy he followed when he became President. He would permit the federal courts to suspend operation if necessary, and Southerners could go without mail service if they wanted to. Moreover, there would be no invasion, no use of force, except (and this is a big exception) what may be necessary to "hold, occupy, and possess the property and places belonging to the government, and to collect the duties and imposts." This being the case, I do not interpret Lincoln's statement that he would uphold the laws as "purely a declaration of principle, with no operative or functional meaning" as Professor Potter does. I believe that Lincoln was as precise in his statements here as Professor Potter has found him to be elsewhere.

I see no evidence that Lincoln became increasingly receptive to the idea of voluntary reunion during the month of February. Professor Potter describes what was happening in Virginia, North Carolina, Tennessee, Arkansas, and Missouri, where secession was defeated. But he ignores what was happening in Montgomery, Alabama, where the Confederate States of America took form that very month; the fact that not one of the seceded states sent representatives to the peace conference that was then meeting in Washington; and the fact that the Texas convention, on February 1, approved secession by a vote of 166 to 7. To me, Lincoln's remarks on the way to Washington in February, as well as his inaugural address, indicate that he had come to the disagreeable conclusion that as President he might very well have to use force against the secessionists. Hence he was doing his best to prepare the people for it and to assure them that the responsibility for violence would lay with the South: "In *your* hands, my dissatisfied fellow countrymen, and not in *mine,* is the momentous issue of civil war."

Why, then, did the Republicans reject compromise and peaceful secession? A few, no doubt, because they believed that Southern Unionists would be able to suppress the secessionists by themselves; a few because they could both anticipate and accept the alternative of civil war; most because they were willing to take their chances with the alternative of enforcing the laws.

And why should so many Republicans have preferred the risks of enforcing the laws to compromise or peaceful secession? For a variety of reasons: some because they believed it was a dangerous precedent to compromise with men who were committing treason; some because they thought it was morally wrong to make further concessions to the Slave Power; some because their national pride was deeply offended by the Southern effort to dismember the federal Union; some because they believed that the failure of the American experiment in self-government would dishearten liberal political forces in the whole western world; and some, no doubt, because they were afraid that compromise would destroy the Republican party, as it had destroyed the Whig party.

Lincoln, in his second inaugural address, explained precisely the ultimate consequence of the Republican rejection of both compromise and peaceful secession: "Both parties deprecated war, but one of them would *make* war rather than let the nation survive, and the other would *accept* war rather than let it perish, and the war came."

LIST OF CONTRIBUTORS

AVERY O. CRAVEN is professor of American history at the University of Chicago. He is author of a number of books, among them *The Growth of Southern Nationalism, 1848–1861* (Vol. VI in *A History of the South*), and *Civil War in the Making, 1815–1860*.

DON E. FEHRENBACHER is professor of history at Stanford University. He was a Guggenheim fellow in 1959; he is the author of *Chicago Giant: A Biography of "Long John" Wentworth* and *Prelude to Greatness: Lincoln in the 1850's*.

ROBERT W. JOHANNSEN is professor of history and chairman of the Department of History at the University of Illinois. His books include *Frontier Politics and the Sectional Conflict* and *Letters of Stephen A. Douglas*.

ROY F. NICHOLS is professor of history and vice provost and dean of the Graduate School of Arts and Sciences at the University of Pennsylvania. He won the Pulitzer Prize in history in 1949 and has written *Disruption of the American Democracy* and *Stakes of Power, 1845–1877*.

DAVID M. POTTER is a Coe professor of American history at Stanford University. Among his books are *Lincoln and His Party in the Secession Crisis* and *Nationalism and Sectionalism in America;* he is co-author of the latter.

CHARLES G. SELLERS, JR., is professor of history at the University of California, Berkeley. He is coeditor of *The Southerner as American*.

KENNETH M. STAMPP is a Morrison professor of American history at the University of California, Berkeley. His recent books include *And the War Came: The North and the Secession Crisis, 1860–1861*, and *The Causes of the Civil War*.

GLYNDON G. VAN DEUSEN is a research professor emeritus at the University of Rochester. He is the author of *The Life of Henry Clay* and *Horace Greeley: Nineteenth Century Crusader*.